Justice or Atrocity

General George E. Pickett
and the Kinston, N.C. Hangings

By Gerard A. Patterson

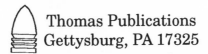

Thomas Publications
Gettysburg, PA 17325

Publisher — Cataloging-in-Publication Data
Patterson, Gerard A.
    Justice or atrocity: General George E. Pickett and the Kinston, NC hangings / Gerard A. Patterson
    160 pp.   15.25 x 22.9 cm.
    Includes index, bibliography.
    ISBN 1-57747-027-3 (Hardbound)
    ISBN 1-57747-042-7 (Softbound)
    1. Confederate States of America—History. 2. United States—History—Civil War, 1861-65—biography, Confederate. 3. Pickett, George Edward 1825-1875 I. Title
E475.97   973.737/P317d   LCC 98-84401

Printed in the United States of America

Published by THOMAS PUBLICATIONS
        P.O. Box 3031
        Gettysburg, Pa. 17325

Cover design by Ryan C. Stouch

To Diane, as always

Table of Contents

Acknowledgements

Information about such an historically obscure incident as the executions that took place in little Kinston, N. C., in 1864 and the far-reaching repercussions must be gleaned in bits and pieces from a large number of widely-spaced sources and assembled to be appreciated.

In my research forays, I have been aided immeasurably by the staffs of such institutions as the Lenoir Community College library at Kinston, the Virginia Historical Society in Richmond and the manuscript division of the North Carolina Department of Archives and History at Raleigh, as well as by the National Park Service historians at the Petersburg National Battlefield, who were able to direct me to many locations associated with General Pickett's tour of duty at Petersburg, Va., as a department commander.

In response to a telephone inquiry about the availability of certain documents, staffers at the Library of Congress in Washington were kind enough to locate, copy and mail to me the complete transcripts of the two boards of inquiry on the Kinston hangings.

Other individuals who were of special help include John R. Barden, who, though the Kinston affair was hardly in his bailiwick, generously shared with me numerous sources of information he had found while pursuing his own research as historian of the Tryon Palace Restoration Complex at New Bern, N. C.

David M. Sherman of Arlington, Va., graciously provided me with a number of family papers and documents associated with his great-great uncle, Colonel John T. Mercer, C. S. A. George K. Combs of Lloyd House, Library of Virginia History & Genealogy, at Alexandria, Va., sent me copies of the letters of Brigadier General Montgomery Corse, C. S. A. Michael Vouri, while with the Whatcom Museum of History and Art in Bellingham, Wa., filled in many details of Pickett's prewar service in the Pacific Northwest. For several years, I have had the benefit of comparing notes

on Pickett's career with someone who has made it something of a life's work, Dr. Richard Selcer of Fort Worth, Tx.

I would be remiss if I did not also thank the knowledgeable staff of the public library of Mt. Lebanon, Pa., where I reside, for obtaining numerous tough-to-find works for me through the interlibrary lending service, saving me much time and expense.

The work has been much improved by the editing skill and historical knowledge of Sarah Sites Rodgers, editor at Thomas Publications.

Finally, I must again thank my wife Diane for the many ways she has helped bring this study to completion, from copy reading to encouraging me to continue when progress became imperceptibly slow.

To all these groups and individuals, I am most appreciative.

Gerard A. Patterson

Sherman has correctly said that war is hell, and it really looked it, with all those men being hung and shot, as if hell had broke loose in North Carolina.

Captain John G. Smith
8th Georgia Cavalry, C. S. A.

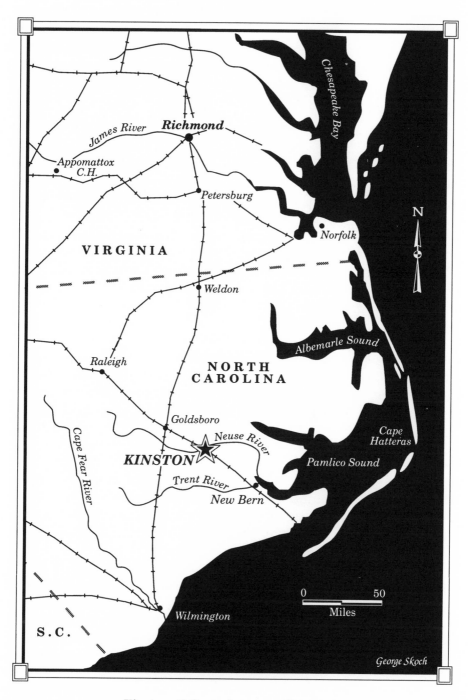

Kinston, N.C., and surrounding area.

Introduction

Twenty-two men. Factored in the grand tally of Civil War deaths—an addition of more than a half-million men—what significance could the loss of this handful of simple, unschooled rustics from the pine bogs of coastal North Carolina hold?

They were deserters, duly executed for their crime like hundreds of others in that war in the interest of maintaining military discipline. What set apart the hanging of this sorry set in Kinston, N. C., in the gray winter of 1864 was that the condemned wore Union army uniforms and were sentenced by Confederate authorities for having left the Rebel camp.

Irony is a subtlety that none of these men was intellectually conditioned to appreciate, yet their singular situation reflected some of the most unlikely behavior imaginable by a cast just as improbable, an assemblage that included a number of officials of far more prominence than the victims could ever have thought they would attract.

As they stood on the roughly-fashioned scaffold about to be launched into eternity over a matter of loyalty—with rough corn sacks over their heads in lieu of the prescribed black hoods—it is hardly likely that that word occupied their final thoughts. Their deaths, however, would raise many troubling questions about the true definition of "loyalty" and, in the context of what would be officially regarded as the War of the Rebellion, what obligation is implicit in it.

For in the final analysis, these indifferent soldiers were being put to death for, however belatedly, professing their allegiance to a country which their executioners had themselves abandoned to form a new one of their own. The Confederate leaders carrying out the sentences (at a time when their wavering ranks desperately needed stiffening) included a number of West Point graduates and former U. S. Army officers who had themselves once sworn a solemn oath of loyalty to the U. S. government. Indeed, the man directly responsible for their court martial and who had approved their death sentences—Major General George E. Pickett, C. S. A.—owed his own

appointment to the U. S. Military Academy to the current president of the United States, Abraham Lincoln.

Loyalty? If it were something that these, for the main, illiterate North Carolinians had been expected to render this newly-formed Confederate government because wealthy John Washington of Kinston and some others with an economic or political stake had gotten together at Raleigh and adopted articles of secession, it was a proposition that overlooked the fact that their interest in governmental structures was as scanty as their understanding of them. Whatever sectional discord existed between Northern and Southern states could in no discernible way relate to their own base and secluded existence. If they recognized any responsibility, it was to use whatever common sense they possessed to find ways to avoid being taken away from their bare board, ramshackle homes and near-worthless acres into a distant quarrel that defied their comprehension.

Loyalty? Even though so uncompromisingly demanded of such men as these, it proved to be an elusive concept later to others far more schooled and intelligent when efforts were made to bring the hangmen to account for what had taken place at Kinston.

Then, we find even high Federal officials like General Ulysses S. Grant, commander of the U. S. Army, giving the quality odd dimensions as they anguished to balance their personal loyalty to "old army" chums like Pickett with their duty to deal with the murder of 22 citizens of the United States not of their professional clique.

But the Kinston affair is also a model study of other social conflicts that have somehow been overlooked or denigrated in the overwhelming effort to simplify what was in reality an infinitely complex struggle. It brought out, for example, the social schism that existed between soldiers of the various Confederate states, underscoring the utter disdain with which Virginians were capable of regarding North Carolinians, and vice-versa.

It showed how an orderly, resourceful river town could be changed by war into a vice-ridden Sodom of the South, alternately accommodating the soldiers of one army and then the other, and how its inhabitants could grow to accept the most shocking occurrences within their midst without protest or complaint. And in the cruel, heartless manner in which the Kinston executions were carried out, it repeated history's oft-presented lesson of how barbaric even the deeply religious can behave when encouraged and protected by authority, no matter how dubious that source.

The affair is noteworthy for the procession of diverse characters it involved. They ranged from the mysterious cross-eyed executioner

who took the clothing of the victims as his pay, to the fanatical minister who baptized the condemned men in the nearby Neuse River before escorting them unforgiven to the scaffold. But none was more enigmatic than Pickett himself, a strange blend of gushy sentimentality and ruthlessness. An officer whose name will forever be associated with the grand, climactic assault on Cemetery Ridge at Gettysburg—Pickett's Charge—the high-bred Virginian might well have found himself on trial as a war criminal for his conduct in North Carolina. Though his own dedication to duty frequently lapsed, he became a man virtually obsessed with the punishment of desertion regardless of motivation.

The moral and legal issues that the Kinston executions raised were intriguing and unsettling. If they felt their actions justified, the Confederate officers involved seemed to carefully avoid mentioning the event in their official reports as well as their memoirs. Even the court martial records that sent the convicted men to the gallows disappeared.

The incident is one that challenges each individual evaluating it to exercise a personal sense of justice and conclude whether or not a gross offense was permitted to go unpunished. It is not an easy verdict to reach. Lingering about the deliberations is always the troublesome question of whether, ultimately, these 22 young men were simply the victims of the ambiguity inherent in such lofty words as loyalty.

Major General George E. Pickett

CHAPTER ONE

Opportunity at New Bern

It was the supreme moment of George E. Pickett's life.

As the stocky yet graceful horseman moved about his Virginia troops—readying themselves on the concealed side of a long ridge dominated by a Lutheran seminary and out of sight, for the moment, of the blue figures fringing the broad, green and amber expanse of Pennsylvania farmland over which they would soon have to advance—several of the men noted how jaunty and high-spirited their general appeared. He was dressed as rakishly as usual, a French kepi tilted on the side of his head, his peculiarly long brown curls flowing down to the shoulders of his gray, brass-buttoned and lace trimmed tunic. As he drew close to his rustic volunteers, the scent of the perfumed oils he used to proudly anoint his locks and beard could only remind them of the odoriferous contrast with their own sweaty, unwashed bodies and worn homespun uniforms, and most particularly, their matted, unkempt hair.

But it was the mood of the 38-year-old infantry division commander more than his now-familiar flamboyant appearance that impressed his soldiers. As they rather grimly prepared for their turn in combat—examining their muskets, clustering their blanket rolls and other personal belongings in company piles about a designated tree to be reclaimed when the work was done, or removing the oil-cloth casing from the staffs and shaking out their tightly-furled blue Virginia state banners and the red battleflags intersected with St. Andrew's crosses—some noted how sanguine and pleased with himself the general seemed to be. Indeed, as an artillery officer found in chatting with him, Pickett "thought himself in luck to have the chance."[1]

In the orchard of the Spangler Farm, Pickett's key officers prepared in their own fashion, sitting about in a group gnawing on some cold mutton provided by their commander's old West Point classmate from Tennessee, Brigadier General Cadmus Marcellous Wilcox, and passing around a jug of Pennsylvania whiskey. One of them, Brigadier General Richard Garnett, was ill that July day and though the temperature was in the 90s he was bundled up in his old blue

overcoat from the regular army. At some point, Garnett limped up to get a view of the far-off Union line on Cemetery Ridge and was heard to mutter, "This is a desperate thing to attempt."[2]

But Pickett had no such pessimistic thoughts. Never mind the distance. Confident in his division, sure of support as promised, Pickett excitedly awaited his opportunity to be the officer who broke the Federal center at Gettysburg, and the honor which would surely follow that achievement.

There had not been that many opportunities of late for either Pickett or his men. John Bell Hood and his Texans, A. P. Hill and the Light Division, now under Dorsey Pender—these were the commanders and the units that had gained fame while Pickett had been convalescing with a shoulder wound received during the Seven Days the year before. His troops had not seen heavy action since Sharpsburg, had missed Chancellorsville while on detached service gathering provisions around Suffolk and the Blackwater region. Given a choice, it is unlikely that Pickett would have been the first of his lieutenants chosen by Lee for this mission, but this was the only unused infantry force he had left. Determined as he was to go through with this attack, it would have to be Pickett's Division, along with Major General Henry Heth's and some of Pender's men, already in position in that sector though they had really done more than their share of fighting.

At about 3 p.m., a salvo from a section of the Washington Artillery served as the signal for the preparatory barrage of the Union line to begin. In a moment, more than 100 guns would be pounding away in scattered, discordant fashion, giving little clue to the intended point of attack. Union gunners responded with an even louder voice. Along with the unnerving din, both sides found themselves contributing to the formation of a choking, eye-smarting sulfurous haze over the open field.

The cannonade had gone on for nearly an hour when the excited, proud Pickett cantored up to his corps commander and longtime friend, Lieutenant General James Longstreet. Both were out of West Point, though "Pete" Longstreet was a few years older. They had been to Mexico together and later served with the 8th Infantry at Jefferson Barracks with U. S. "Sam" Grant before duty sent Pickett to the Pacific Northwest for a long stretch. Though there was nothing of Pickett's showiness about the bulky Longstreet, a man whose own dress was distinguished mainly for the number of buttons he had missing, and nothing as affected or pretentious about this gruff, earthy man, he rather inexplicably thought the world of George

Pickett. This closeness was evident now when Pickett said to him, "I shall take my division forward, sir." Longstreet, seeing the situation far more clearly and darkly doubtful that the assault Lee had ordered could succeed, could not speak, and merely nodded.[3]

Pickett galloped back to his regiments and sang out, "Up, men, and to your posts. Don't forget today that you are from Old Virginia."[4] By the thousands, gray and brown-clad riflemen began to filter out of the thicket that had given them some cover during the bombardment and, in response to the bellowing of their officers, started to elbow and nudge themselves into several seemingly endless lines that gradually disappeared in the smoke hanging over the ground like a morning mist. Most of Pickett's men were unaware that a formation even larger than their own was gathering at a further point down the ridge and would converge with them when the advance began to form an amalgamated force of more than 13,000 infantrymen. Their riddled flags with small strips of ribbon bearing the names of battles haphazardly sewn on, brandished by their brazen bearers, gave little dots of swirling color to the long gray lines and enabled the far-off Federal soldiers lining Cemetery Ridge to estimate the number of regiments being hurled against them.

"Sergeant, are you going to put those colors on the enemy's works today?" Brigadier General Lewis Armistead called out to the standard bearer of the 53rd Virginia.

"I will try, sir," he responded, "and if mortal man can do it, it shall be done."[5]

Finally, Pickett roared "Division, forward." The order, in military fashion, was relayed down the ranks, repeated by regimental colonels to company captains—first the preparatory command to summon attention, "regiment," with the captains responding, "company," and then the command of execution reverberating somewhat more in chorus, "Forward." The unwieldy conglomeration lurched ahead, soon losing any precise alignment but moving in a series of great, inexorable waves. Here and there, the somber, rhythmic tapping on drums sought to set a pace. For direction, the officers had been told to focus on a small group of young trees conspicuously clustered in the open ground in the center of the Federal position. The privates relied on the battle flags to guide them, and to indicate just how far duty demanded they advance and when they could honorably withdraw.

As the attack began, nervous, high-strung Cadmus Wilcox rode up to Pickett, offered him his flask and said, "Take a drink with me—in an hour you'll be in hell or glory."[6] A man hardly adverse to

a dram himself, Pickett declined, either because he felt intoxicated enough by his role in these events, or he did not sense the personal peril that Wilcox imagined. Curiously, one of his privates noted that Pickett, "rather dandyish in his ruffles and curls" appeared "ready to ride to death if need be," and seemed also to assume that the general would be in the thick of things.[7] But Pickett had no intention of actually leading this charge.

As the lines surged onward, the general and his staff lagged behind. When the roaring, howling troops rushed across the Emmitsburg Road that cut through the field, halfway to their objective, Pickett halted by the red barn of the Codori Farm at the roadside and made that his field headquarters. From there he could observe the progress of the battle, though there was little more that he could do now to influence the outcome.

The whole thing took but a few minutes to resolve. What Pickett saw developing through his field glasses soon began to unnerve him. The lines began to break, and fall apart. To cross a mile of open ground had been too much to ask of any infantry exposed to solid shot, then musketry and grape and canister discharged so rapidly the Union gunners did not even pause to swab the barrels. More devastatingly, Federal troops had worked their way around to the Rebel's right flank and it was crumbling under the crossfire. The brigade commanders and colonels who had gone forward with their men tried to urge them on when they saw some hesitate in fear as their ranks began to rapidly thin under the torrent while others, who could control themselves no longer, halted just to fire back.

A riderless black charger, bleeding heavily from wounds and stumbling madly about the field, indicated to Pickett that his friend Garnett was down. One horde of men crowded about a bareheaded officer wildly waving a sword, on the tip of which a gray felt hat had been placed to give direction but had slid down the blade through a rent to the hilt. Armistead. Pickett could see "Old Lew" among the guns. Sensing that there was still a chance, he sent not one but three couriers in succession, racing back to Wilcox summoning him to reinforce the men with his Alabama brigade. But it was useless; the attack was a failure. Thousands of men began to signal surrender on the slope, or were dropping their weapons and scampering back across the field to their own lines. Banners by the dozen were left littering the ground with no one left with enough heart to raise them.

Pickett broke down as he saw his great opportunity ruined. He began to cry; tears streamed down his florid face as he spurred his horse and galloped away from the farm back to Seminary Ridge.

His long hair blowing crazily in the breeze, he shouted repeatedly for the whereabouts of his friend and protector, Longstreet. When he found the First Corps commander, Pickett's exclamation betrayed his consuming concern: "General, I am ruined. My division is gone—it is destroyed."[8]

Sobbing heavily, he moved about the mob of returning stragglers and implored, "Great God, where, oh where is my division?"[9] At some point, Pickett came upon General Lee, who tried to console him by saying, "This has been my fight, and upon my shoulders rests the blame."[10] It was an admission to which Pickett would always hold Lee.

In military annals, it would go down as Pickett's Charge, a grand, heroic effort that failed. But to George Pickett, it was an embittering, personal defeat, one from which he would never recover. The pain and trauma he experienced would stay with him and render him, as a troop commander, forever shaken and in dread of further failure. But more than anything else, Gettysburg made him an angry, almost vicious man.

On the slow, tortuous retreat back to Virginia, during which Pickett had the inglorious assignment of escorting a procession of Union prisoners almost as large as his shattered division, the disconsolate general let his feelings about the campaign leak out through his pen. His correspondent was a bright-eyed product of the Lynchburg Academy to whom he was, despite the generational gap between them, engaged to be married. Her name was LaSalle Corbell—Sally.

Just what he wrote on this occasion or others, is a matter of deserved suspicion. For when the recipient decided years later to share her chest of love letters from the man she unabashedly worshipped they were revealed in heavily edited form. Rarely did she produce the originals for scrutiny, raising questions of their very existence. But one phrase in Pickett's post-Gettysburg letter is particularly intriguing. After describing his losses in the charge, he supposedly added, "How I escaped it is a miracle."[11] Either Pickett amplified his conduct to impress his sweetheart or Sally attempted to embellish the performance of the man she adored.

There was, of course, no need for a miracle. Pickett as a division commander with overall responsibility for a large force, had sensibly decided to maintain a safe and secure position of control. There had been a time when Pickett might have plunged into the fray; his West

(Museum of the Confederacy)

General and Mrs. George E. Pickett as newlyweds.

Point chums would always remember him at Chapultepec in Mexico. There, as a young lieutenant, he had boldly seized the colors and rushed forward to plant them on the enemy's works.

Now, in his late 30s, with many years of Indian fighting and frontier service behind him, he no longer chose to expose himself in such foolhardy fashion. Indeed, one of Pickett's colonels noted with some distaste the general's habit of crouching down on his horse's neck when mounted and under fire. Seeing this, the subordinate tried to show him up by sitting upright in the saddle as an example of fearlessness for the enlisted men. At one point during the Union cannonade at Gettysburg, a regimental surgeon saw Pickett "standing behind a large oak tree, holding his horse by the bridle, while his chief of staff, Major [Walter] Harrison was similarly situated a few steps distant." When a shell exploded in a tree over Harrison's head, "both he and Gen. Pickett mounted their horses and rode rapidly to the rear." Asking his acquaintance to keep this information confidential, the physician suggested that they "cover the deficiencies with the mantle of charity."[12]

Yet there was no real question of Pickett's guts, only the degree of his prudence. Probably the best witness that Pickett had of his courage was one of the bluntest, opinionated individuals associated with the First Corps. To the hard-swearing commissary officer, Major Raphael Moses, Pickett was a "very foppish" character, "a dapper little fellow," but, he stressed, "brave as they ever make men."[13]

That Pickett wanted to impress Sally in his letters with his heroics was forgivable enough, for he had become hopelessly infatuated with the Tidewater beauty. That spring, before the Pennsylvania campaign, his division and Hood's had been dispatched under General Longstreet to the Blackwater region on a massive foraging expedition. While a half-hearted siege was conducted against Suffolk to keep the Yankee garrison in check, Major Moses sent his supply wagons every day and depleted the area of its stores of bacon and barreled fish that were available in the coastal towns. "As soon as I advised General Longstreet that the object of the investment had been fully accomplished," the scavenger recalled, "the siege was raised."[14] No one could have been more disappointed to see the operation concluded than Pickett, for his precious Sally resided in that vicinity and had commanded more of his attention than his division.

"Pickett's visits were frequent, a long night ride and return for duty early next day," Longstreet's chief of staff, Moxley Sorrel recalled of his forays. "Perhaps he had wearied Longstreet by frequent applications to be absent, but once he came to me for the

authority. My answer was, 'No, you must go to the lieutenant general.'

"'But he is tired of it, and will refuse; and I must go, I must see her. I swear, Sorrel, I'll be back before anything can happen in the morning.'

"I could not permit myself to be moved. If anything did happen, such as a movement of his division or any demonstration against it, my responsibility for the absence of the major general could not be explained. But Pickett went all the same, nothing could hold him back from that pursuit...I don't think his division benefitted by such carpet-knight doings in the field."[15]

Just how old was the object of the smitten general's affection is a matter much confused by the lady herself. In her writings, she indicated that she was but 14 at the time of the Suffolk campaign. Yet there exists convincing evidence that after the war, she adjusted her age backward and that she was actually about 19 years old at this time.

Despite Sally's tender years, theirs had been something of a lengthy as well as bizarre relationship. She had first set eyes on George Pickett at the Virginia seashore in the summer of 1852. He was on leave and mourning the loss of his first wife, Sallie Minge of Richmond, who had died suddenly in November, 1851, only eleven months after their marriage and while he was stationed in Texas.

Sally Corbell recalled her first meeting with her soldier quite vividly:

> One morning, while playing alone on the beach, I saw an officer lying on the sand reading, under the shelter of an umbrella. I had noticed him several times, always apart from the others, and very sad. I could imagine but one reason for his desolation and in pity for him, I crept under the umbrella to ask him if he, too, had the whooping cough. He smiled and answered no, but as I still persisted he drew me to him, telling me that he had lost someone who was dear to him and he was very lonely...Child as I was, I believe I lost my heart to him on the spot. At all events, I crept from under the umbrella pledged to Lieutenant George E. Pickett, U. S. A., for life and death.[16]

Of his appearance, what particularly impressed her was the neatness of his dress:

> His shirtfront of the finest white linen, was in soft puffs and ruffles, and the sleeves were edged with hemstitched thread cambric ruffles. He would never, to the end of his life, wear the

stiff linen collars and cuffs and stocks which came into fashion among men. While he was at West Point he paid heavily in demerits for obstinacy in refusing to wear the regulation stock. Only when the demerits reached the danger point would he temporarily give up his soft necktie.[17]

Their meeting under the beach umbrella ended with him giving Sally a tiny ring and locket which she cherished.[18] Three years later, they met again. He had just received his commission as captain and was recruiting his company at Fort Monroe before sailing for the Washington Territory: "The first real sorrow of my life was when I watched the St. Louis go out to sea with my soldier on board, bound around the Horn to Puget Sound, where he was stationed at Fort Bellingham, which I thought must be farther than the end of the world."[19] When he would return, neither of them had any idea.

In the great pine-tipped Northwest, still sparsely settled and unspoiled, Pickett quickly became immersed in the culture of the local tribes. He learned to speak Chinook, built schoolhouses for the children, and earned the appellation Nesika Tyee—Our Chief. But it was lonely duty for a young officer and after some months Pickett took up with a Haida Indian girl. Though his long-established family at Turkey Island near Richmond would hardly have been overjoyed at the news, Pickett decided to marry his dark-skinned companion. They were joined in a tribal rite and moved into a comfortable frame house near the unthreatened fort, where the bride was always respectfully referred to as Mrs. Pickett. On December 31, 1857, their son was born. He was named James Tilton Pickett, after close friend Major James Tilton, adjutant general of the territorial volunteers.

Tragically, this second wife also died soon after their child arrived and Pickett was left with the responsibility of raising the boy alone. The burden proved too much for the young captain and in 1859 he arranged to have Jimmie cared for by a childless couple named Mr. and Mrs. William Collins who lived on a farm near the small trading center of Arcadia.[20]

That year, Pickett came home on a leave of several months and on a visit to White Sulphur Spring happened to encounter Sally and her family once more, vacationing at the Greenbriar. "Though still a child, I held that he was pledged to me and resented his attentions to the belles nearer his own age," Sally later related. "Amused and pleased by this, he humored me...by dancing in the evening with no one but me until the children's bed time came when the ballroom was reluctantly given up to the grown people. One Baltimore beauty took my soldier to task for

his bad taste in dancing with a child, thereby canceling the little friendship which had existed between them."[21]

How much Pickett chose to relate about his Indian marriage in Washington Territory or its offspring to his young admirer is uncertain. But when he returned from his furlough to his 9th Infantry company, little Sally was clearly more infatuated with him than ever.

As remote as the Pacific Northwest was from the eye of the sectional storm about to erupt, a group of political leaders there was sufficiently concerned to attempt to create a diversion that might distract the nation from its course. According to George B. McClellan, what they had in mind was stirring up a border dispute with Great Britain and making possession of San Juan Island in Puget Sound the object of controversy. The civil authorities found Captain Pickett a willing co-conspirator, ready on his own hook to lend his troops and his flag to the intimidation. With a single company, he made much of a show by daring a British fleet to seize the island. The matter was resolved without a shot being exchanged and without inflaming warlike passions either in Washington, D. C., or London as had supposedly been hoped by the agitators. But the episode brought a good deal of national press attention to Pickett for his heroic posture and Congress tendered a resolution of commendation to him.

The approaching civil war caught Pickett in a predicament somewhat different than that of other Southern officers in the army, one he was not sure how to handle. He considered himself a Virginian but by a quirk of circumstance he owed his appointment to West Point, indirectly, to the man who had just been elected president of the United States—Abraham Lincoln.

Longing to enter the U.S. Military Academy, Pickett found his state's quota filled. He determined to establish residency in Illinois, where his mother's brother, Andrew Johnston, had relocated and was practicing law, in the hope of gaining an appointment from that state. Then just seventeen, he moved to Quincy where he became acquainted with his uncle's legal associate, young Mr. Lincoln. Much taken by the spirited lad (who occupied much of his time in Quincy performing with a local theater group) Lincoln soon interceded with U.S. Representative John G. Stuart of the Third Illinois District to secure Pickett's appointment to the academy and started him on his army career.

Regardless of his status or culpability for future charges of desertion, when Virginia seceded Pickett was determined to end his long association with the U. S. Army and return to Richmond. To cover his departure, he concocted a story about his being left a legacy and having to return promptly to Virginia to settle his business.

Before leaving on his phony emergency leave, Pickett undertook to put his affairs in order. From "Camp Pickett, San Juan Island," he wrote to an acquaintance in Olympia on July 2, 1861:

> *Dear Goldsborough,*
>
> *Having applied for a leave of absence and being in expectation of leaving this country very shortly, I here-with enclose an order on you to pay the amount of $100 to Major James Tilton. Tilton has been kind enough to look after the welfare of my little boy, and will during my absence continue to take care of him. It is for this purpose that I give him the order.*[22]

Tilton did indeed take almost a fatherly interest in Jimmie's well-being and was in frequent touch with the Collins family, often relaying news of Pickett to them. On August 8, for example, he wrote from Olympia:

> *Captain Pickett passed through here a few days since on his way to Virginia, he having resigned his commission in the army. He bid me say good-bye to Mr. Collins, yourself, and the boy. He regrets much that he could not take time to come down, but he was on a 30 day leave and had to reach Washington City in that time, so he went through via St. Louis and Sacramento and Portland, overland.*
>
> *He hopes some other time to come out here again and promises to write to me as soon as he can. I hope this Civil War will stop soon. He sent his bible, his commission and his leave of absence for his boy that the youngster might know who his father was, and should Pickett be killed, his aunt in Virginia will look out for him.*[23]

At some point, Pickett decided it would be less risky for him to travel by sea than overland and altered his plans. He sailed on a merchant vessel down the Pacific Coast, crossed the Isthmus of Panama, and on landing in New York aboard another ship, disguised himself and made his way up to Canada and finally reached Richmond by way of Kentucky, months after the first battle of Manassas had been fought.

Waiting anxiously for his arrival was Sally Corbell, old enough now to stir Pickett to the point of distraction. When separated by her academy studies or his campaigns, a steady stream of syrupy prose flowed between them. Besides showing her affection in letters, Sally pandered to his sartorial tastes by gorgeously embroidering his cape, the stars on his tunic, and even his carpet slippers.

Just as her image of her soldier's celibate life out in the Northwest may have been somewhat distorted, so obviously was her understanding of how Pickett pursued his profession. She appeared to assume that the sensitive manner and gentle demeanor he showed her were no different than those adopted with the men with whom he served in the army. In that, Sally was as blind as anyone ever smitten. She could not see, or chose not to accept the reality that, away from her, Pickett was a different man. He was an officer with a very clear, cold, traditional view of the juxtaposition of superior and subordinate in military life. Sally understandably preferred to think of him as deeply beloved by his fellow officers and the men in his ranks. Their attachment to him, she averred, was something phenomenal and equaled only by his devotion to them.

Actually, Pickett never—from the beginning of the war—formed that sort of relationship with the men under his command. It was one he could neither engender nor tolerate. Pickett, in fact, very quickly categorized himself as something of a spit-and-polish martinet of the type the informal rustics in the ranks so much disliked. Private Randolph A. Shotwell of the 8th Virginia recalled the day his unit was inspected for the first time by its new commander:

> *He is an old West Pointer and conducted himself accordingly. Taking up my gun, he rubbed his white glove over the barrel and lo! A rusty streak on the glove! For some unaccountable reason Col. [Eppa] Hunton came in front of me and said: "General, this young man left college at the North to come South and fight with us. Pickett whipped out his handkerchief and blew a nasal blast...only this and nothing more.*[24]

Such gestures of disdain were hardly likely to endear an officer to those under his control. But Sally had her own image of her beau and probably did not notice in his appearance what was evident to a Union prisoner who got a glimpse of Pickett at Gettysburg on the morning before the charge:

> *The archetype of a Virginia slave baron strutted briskly, proud in bearing, head lifted in arrogance. On horseback he looked like the ruler of a continent. Obviously he took pains with appearance—riding boots aglitter, near-shoulder-length hair tonsorially styled—but the color of his nose and upper cheeks betrayed that he pandered the inner man. Pleasures of the bottle left indelible tracks. Indeed the coarse plebian features in no way matched the efforts at aristocratic airs.*[25]

Similarly, while Sally delighted in her general's tender letters to her and his sweet references to "my little one," she might well have been taken aback by the biting tone he could adopt in his official correspondence. General Lee witnessed Pickett in full rage after the Pennsylvania campaign and was so shocked by his criticism of the conduct of others during the disastrous charge that he took the extraordinary step of ordering the general to withdraw the report:

> *You and your men have crowned themselves with glory; but we have the enemy to fight, and must carefully, at this critical moment, guard against dissensions which the reflections in your report would create. I will, therefore, suggest that you destroy both copy and original, substituting one confined to casualties merely. I hope all will yet be well.*[26]

While he reluctantly took back the account, Pickett did not destroy it as suggested. Though it went no further, the exchange with Lee illustrated still another aspect of the multifaceted nature of this unusual man who was perceived in so many different ways by those he encountered. He was anxious to protect his reputation, and willing to point to others when things went awry.

After the defeated army arrived back in Virginia, there was high-level concern expressed over what best to do about rebuilding Pickett's battered remnant. He had lost more than half his force at Gettysburg, including seven colonels killed. Only one field grade officer in the entire division—aside from himself—had escaped the charge unscathed. Endorsing the suggestion of his First Corps commander, General Lee notified President Jefferson Davis from Orange Court House on September 9, 1863:

> *General Longstreet proposes that Pickett's division take the place of Wise's and Jenkins' brigades about Richmond and that they accompany him (to Tennessee). Pickett's division wants many officers, owing to the number wounded and captured, who cannot now be replaced. He also thinks it might increase its ranks in that locality....*[27]

Jefferson Davis concurred with this trade of units. Not only was his division to be given a chance to recuperate in a quiet sector by serving as a reserve force for the defense of the capital, but Pickett gained an impressive new title that carried with it some vague, as yet undefined responsibility. Special Order No. 226 from the adjutant and inspector general's office in Richmond stated simply: "Maj.

Gen. George E. Pickett, Provisional Army, C. S., is assigned to the command of the Department of North Carolina, headquarters at Petersburg, Va."[28]

That the commander of the Department of North Carolina should be directed to maintain headquarters in Petersburg, 22 miles from Richmond and more than twice that to the state line, was not really as inappropriate as it appeared because his area of responsibility actually began at the Blackwater River and included all of southeast Virginia. Pickett was, no doubt, aware of the troubled conditions in North Carolina, with many of its seacoast towns—including Plymouth and New Bern—long occupied by the Federals and used as bases for incursions deep into the state. Undisciplined squads of Union soldiers—black and white—roamed about looting homes and terrorizing residents while thousands of Confederate deserters formed in bands and defied authorities to approach their seamy camps. With virtually all their own troops serving with Lee in Virginia, state authorities were powerless to cope with the demoralizing and deteriorating situation. How Pickett was expected to deal with it and with what resources, he had still no idea.

But these problems were remote from pleasant old Petersburg, so far unharmed by the war. Pickett was confident that he and his men would not be called upon for any hard service until they had a chance to recover and began to make themselves comfortable for a quiet, uneventful winter. Pickett decided that it was time to once more plunge into the sea of matrimony, and only weeks after his assignment sent members of his staff to quiet Chuckatuck to fetch Sally Corbell and her parents, while he arranged for a ceremony at venerable St. Paul's Church in Petersburg, as well as for an appropriate reception to follow in Richmond. When Sally looked back upon the nuptials, the event grew in her mind as most things did. "A salute of a hundred guns announced the marriage; cheers followed us, and chimes and bands and bugles played as we left for our wedding reception in Richmond," she would later write.[29]

The details of the gathering at the capital, not overly dispirited by the outcome of the Pennsylvania campaign, also remained vivid to Sally and gave an indication of Pickett's lofty station in that society:

> *The food supply of the South was reduced to narrow limits then. Salt was reclaimed from the earth under smoke-houses. Guests at distinguished functions were regaled with ice cream made of frozen buttermilk sweetened with sorghum. But friends of the general had almost worked miracles to prepare a wed-*

ding supper. It was sora season, and those little birds had been killed at night with paddles—the South being not much richer in ammunition than in edibles—and contributed so lavishly to our banquet that it was always afterward known as "the wedding sora supper."

Our wedding present from Mrs. Lee was a fruitcake, and Bishop Dudley's mother sent a black cake she had been saving for her golden wedding. Little bags of salt and sugar were sent as presents. The army was in camp nearby and all the men at the reception, except President Davis, his cabinet, and a few clergymen, came in full uniform, officers and privates as well.[30]

There was no opportunity for a wedding trip. That evening, the newlyweds returned by the rickety railroad to Petersburg where they took up residence at the tall, rectangular and spacious McIlwaine House on Washington and Perry streets with its immense shuttered windows and ornate trim that extended to the formation of an elaborate wooden arch atop the steep steps leading to the imposing entrance. An iron fence enclosed the property, about which the bride could see as she arrived a number of sturdy old trees, now bare as the flower beds were barren, and even a gently spouting fountain. It was a lovely setting for her to indulge her passion for prose.

Pickett located his headquarters at the nearby Customs House and post office, a sturdy, gray-stone structure with three arched doorways in front. Lee himself did not have such an impressive command post. Pickett's offices were situated on the second floor and while the mails were sorted and distributed below, a procession of officers and couriers filed up and down a wide staircase to deal with the department commander, for the moment satisfied with the trappings he so much required.

No sooner had Pickett settled in, however, than a rather startling rumor reached him early in October that his division was again to be placed into active service. His alarm was evident in the hastily written note he rushed off to the white-haired, 65-year-old adjutant and inspector general in Richmond, Samuel Cooper, with whom he was soon to become much involved.

I have just learned from General [Seth] Barton that a telegram arrived last night from General Longstreet, calling for my division. It is proper that I should state to you before any movement is made the condition of the command. There have been some few conscripts assigned to us since our arrival in the neighborhood, say 100. At this time there are two officers, one

noncommissioned officer, and three privates absent on recruiting service from each regiment, making 40 officers and 80 privates. The plan of reorganizing this shattered division is in fact but just commenced.

The steps I have taken to gather up the numbers of men on detailed service in and about Richmond are in progress, but should we move now it will be with ranks not recruited, and in fact in no better condition than upon our arrival. The object for which we were left here has not been carried out. In time I will be able to get the division together and in fighting trim; it most emphatically is not so now. And until the ranks are filled up and some more officers promoted to learn some little of their duties, it will not be the crack division it was, and I decidedly would not like to go into action with it....

Why not let this division remain till it is fit for service?[31]

Whether Pickett's entreaty worked or not, the division was not disturbed at that time and his men were beginning to thoroughly enjoy their tranquil location, roaming the well-worn, tree-lined streets, admiring the red brick houses with their small white pillars in front. They loitered about the Petersburg Exchange down by the Appomattox that was crowded with farm wagons laden with produce for the wholesalers, and observed the tobacco auctions on Sycamore Street, somewhat subdued now with the Yankees blockading the ports and limiting shipment, but still the main commercial activity in the town of 18,000 people. Fraternization with the daughters of the local gentry, and the droves of seamstresses who sewed uniforms, sheets and tents at the numerous mills in the community, had become so free that it was decided to relocate the camps a bit more distantly. Consequently, a number of units found themselves moved to the outskirts of the city and stabled at Hare's Race Track. A member of the Fayette Artillery of Richmond, E. W. Gaines, said that his battery mates were so "nicely fixed that they entertained strong hopes it would be a long time ere they would have to take another long march, or participate in some hard struggle.[32]

But less than two months later, and apparently without Pickett's knowledge, some new and ambitious plans were made for the immediate employment of the general and his understrength division with scant regard for the worsening winter weather. In highly secret correspondence with President Davis, General Lee professed on January 2, 1864 that "the time is at hand when, if an attempt can be made to capture the enemy's forces at New Bern, it should be done."

"I can now spare troops for the purpose which will not be the case as spring approaches," he reasoned. Moreover, the garrison at the fortified port some 200 miles distant "has been so unmolested, and experiences such a feeling of security, that it is represented as careless," Lee advised. The general's purpose in urging the expedition was simple: "A large amount of provisions and other supplies are said to be at New Bern, which are much wanted for this army, besides much that is reported in the country that will thus be made accessible to us."[33]

But in approving the plan, the harried president's thoughts must also have encompassed the political implications of such an operation. Conditions in North Carolina were worsening. Opposition to the authority of the Confederate government was becoming more flagrant. A genuine threat existed that elements seeking a negotiated peace with Washington would succeed in pulling the state out of the Confederacy.

The cry of states' rights that had been raised so defiantly against the Union in North Carolina was now the rallying cry for resistance to the Confederate government, particularly when it came to conscription and providing troops for out-of-state service. The challenge of Richmond's right to conscript extended to the chief justice of the Supreme Court of North Carolina, Richmond Mumford Pearson, who had decided that the conscription law was unconstitutional and honored every single request for a writ of habeas corpus submitted on behalf of soldiers arrested for desertion from the Confederate army. This rendered military authorities powerless to deal with the now endemic problem.

Every bit as damaging was the work of the seditious editor of the Raleigh *Standard*, William Woods Holden, who was doing his utmost in the editorial columns of his widely-read newspaper to undermine the central government. His recurring theme was that the conflict had been turned into a "rich man's war, poor man's fight." He cited as his most convincing evidence the Confederate Conscription Act of 1862 that provided for substitutions and the exemption of any man who owned more than 20 slaves. Holden went so far as to encourage his readers to organize peace meetings in their communities "to cast about and see if negotiations could not be set on foot for an honorable peace."

Aware of the disaffection toward the Confederate government at home, North Carolina soldiers at the front became similarly discouraged and were deserting by squads and companies. Typical of the encouragement they were getting to give it up and come home was

the letter one member of the 64th North Carolina Volunteers received from his wife that read:

> *You said you hadn't anything to eat. I wish you was here to get some beans for dinner. I have plenty to eat as yet... The people is generally well hereat. The people is all turning to Union here since the Yankees has got Vicksburg. I want you to come home as soon as you can after you git this letter. Jane Elkins is living with me yet. That is all I can think of only I want you to come home the worst that I ever did. The conscripts is all at home yet, and I don't know what they will do with them. The folks is leaving here and going North as fast as they can. So I will close.[34]*

In some counties, so many deserters congregated in such force that conscript officers dared not try to interfere with them. In Cherokee County, they took over a town and in Wilkes five hundred formed their own regiment and entrenched themselves in a camp and conducted regular drills. They had less trouble subsisting in their own state than when relying on Lee's commissary in Virginia. As one officer said, "while the disaffected feed them from sympathy, the loyal do so from fear."[35]

Federal authorities sensed the opportunity to capitalize on the waning morale of the North Carolinians and Union officers began to recruit citizens in the occupied portions of their state, including deserters from the Confederate forces, and particularly those from the poorer classes who felt they had little stake in the success of the secession movement. President Lincoln's general amnesty offer issued that December to those who would take the oath of allegiance was having an alarming impact. Something had to be done to restore faith in the viability of the government in Richmond and the prospect of eventual victory. Driving the Yankees from one of the most important towns they had long held on the Carolina coast might provide that degree of reassurance. A sizeable force of regular Confederate troops in that part of the state might also help with the rounding up of deserters and discourage any further exodus from the Southern ranks. At any rate, Jefferson Davis readily accepted the proposal for such an attempt.

It was almost three weeks later that the scheme was revealed, in a rather unusual manner, to the man who would have to carry it out. An extremely young brigadier arrived unaccompanied at Pickett's

headquarters from the Army of Northern Virginia's winter encampment on the Rapidan. A stranger to Pickett, there was an extraordinary quality about Robert F. Hoke. In some way, the young North Carolinian commanded instant attention at all levels, from the simple, impressionable youths in the ranks to the mature political and military commanders, although his actual attainments in the field had not been all that outstanding.

Major General Robert Hoke, the enterprising North Carolinian.

Hoke had, after briefly attending the Kentucky Military Institute, managed at the age of seventeen both his family's ironworks and its cotton mill at Lincolnton. He was well accustomed to supervising men far older than himself. Enlisting as a lieutenant, he had, without the benefit of regular U. S. Army service to recommend him or any social or political influence to draw on, reached the rank of colonel and command of the 21st North Carolina, in little over a year. Soon afterwards, at age 26, he became the youngest infantry general with Lee, whom he resembled in physique. He had done particularly well at Fredericksburg, and did not minimize his performance in his official report. A severe shoulder wound received at Chancellorsville had kept him out of the Gettysburg campaign, and he had only recently returned to his command.

The impressive visitor carried with him a dispatch from General Lee containing the bold plan which it soon became evident Hoke himself had devised. After ensuring their privacy, he passed the secret order to Pickett, who must have read it with intense interest and increasing annoyance.

General: From all the information I have received I think the garrison at New Bern can be captured, and I wish it tried, unless upon close examination you find it impracticable.

You can use for that purpose Barton's, Kemper's, Corse's, and as much of Ransom's brigades as you can draw to that point. I shall send, in addition, Hoke's brigade from this army.

General Hoke is familiar with the vicinity of New Bern, has recently returned from a visit to that country, and it is mainly upon his information that my opinion has been formed. He will hand you this letter, and explain to you the general plan, which at this distance, appears to be the best. You can modify it according to circumstances developed by investigation and your good judgment.

Without his consulting maps, what followed could not have made too much sense to Pickett. It referred to many names and places which were unfamiliar to him:

It is proposed that General Barton shall pass south of Trent River and attack the forces said to be stationed behind Brice's Creek, get possession of the railroad to Beaufort, cut off reinforcements from that quarter, and take the town in reverse. General Hoke will move down between the Trent and the Neuse, endeavor to surprise the troops on Batchelder's Creek, silence

*the guns in the star fort and batteries near the Neuse, and pen-
etrate the town in that direction. Whitford's battalion, or such
other force as may be designated, to move down north of the
Neuse, occupy, if they cannot capture, Fort Anderson, at
Barrington Ferry, and endeavor to take in flank with the batteries the line south of the Neuse, so as to lighten Hoke's work.
The night previous to the land attack, Colonel Wood, of the Navy,
with 200 men in boats, will descend the Neuse, and endeavor to
surprise and capture the gunboats in that river, and by their
aid drive the enemy from their guns....*

It all seemed so complicated, and hardly sounded like Lee at all.
And then Pickett read this caution:

*Everything will depend upon the secrecy, expedition, and
boldness of your movements. General Barton should move first,
and be strong enough to resist any combination of the forces
from New Bern and Beaufort. The cavalry had better accompany him to cut the telegraph and railroad, gain information,
etc. General Hoke with his own brigade should move next, the
force north of the Neuse to keep pace with him....*

After more detailed instructions regarding the employment of
artillery, Lee concluded by emphasizing again the importance of surprise:

*Commit nothing to the telegraph that may disclose your
purpose. You must deceive the enemy as to your purpose,
and conceal it from the citizens. As regards the concentra-
tion of troops, you may put it on the ground of apprehension
of an attack from New Bern. General Hoke will give out that
he is going to arrest deserters and recruit his diminished
regiments.*[36]

Most likely, Pickett's vanity suffered from this order. Never
had he been suspected of Napoleonic genius, having graduated
dead last in his class at West Point. Longstreet had helped his
advancement a good deal. "I could always see how he looked after Pickett," Colonel Sorrel recalled. Staff officers were required
to "give him things very fully; indeed, sometimes stay with him to
make sure he did not get astray."[37] Yet, probably never before had
Pickett been given such precise directions for an operation as his
superior was laying on him now, a step-by-step diagram for a movement he was expected to carry out at some distant place. It was a
deflating situation for a major-general. To make things worse,

the man who had authored the plan was to accompany him. It was an arrangement that could not have pleased Pickett even if he were prepared to undertake a new campaign. And with winter upon them, he was nothing of the sort.

The force to be employed seemed imposing enough on paper—more than 13,000 men. But Pickett was all too conscious of the state of his own brigades, and he probably had no idea that Hoke's North Carolina brigade had suffered a disaster of its own two months prior that rivaled Pickett's at Gettysburg. While Hoke was still absent convalescing with his shoulder wound, his command had been ordered with a Louisiana brigade across a bridge on the Rappahannock. In a sudden thrust, Union forces seized the bridge behind them and the two Confederate units were isolated, and a large portion was taken prisoner. Only the 21st North Carolina, on detached duty, had escaped. The selection of Hoke's Brigade for this New Bern mission was, therefore, dictated as much by the need to recruit its thinned ranks as the fact that Hoke had devised the scheme.

With January temperatures plummeting, the ground hard, and the trees now as gray as their uniforms, Pickett's own men were in no mood to be disturbed from the cozy huts they had built for themselves, and they were convinced that they were secure for the season. The men could hardly have responded enthusiastically when word came that they were to take the field again.

"The members of the company needed rest," gunner Gaines of the Fayette Artillery flatly asserted. "They desired a relaxation from the long marches and severe struggles so recently undergone but orders during war are inexorable; so to the work the men went."[38]

Two of the designated infantry brigades had been in the charge at Gettysburg—James Kemper's, now under an oft-wounded colonel who had been to the Virginia Military Institute and had later become a merchant, 36-year-old William R. Terry. The other was Armistead's old command, directed by an intelligent professional soldier from Virginia named Seth Barton, who had been admitted to the U.S. Military Academy at the age of 15 and had seen long service out West before the war. Now 34 and a brigadier, Barton had only recently been exchanged after having been captured at Vicksburg on the day after Pickett's Charge. Corse's Brigade, led by a 47-year-old Alexandria, Virginia banker, Brigadier General Montgomery Corse, had been held back from the Pennsylvania campaign and was for that reason at full strength. Its commander had seen a good deal of combat during the Seven Days and his handsome face was marred by a wound about the mouth he had received at Sharpsburg.

Brigadier General Seth Barton

Pickett's units and the North Carolina troops of Matt Ransom, already in the Petersburg area, would lead the movement south to Kinston, N.C., a town situated 32 miles from New Bern which was to serve as the advanced base for the operation. The troops would not have to march the 160 miles to that jumping off point; it was arranged for them to ride the railroad cars that would otherwise be returning empty to that region via Weldon and Goldsboro after delivering provisions to Lee's army on the Rapidan—from where Hoke's men would be coming.

Two additional regiments that Lee, determined to make sure that Pickett had more than adequate strength to accomplish his mission, had agreed to throw into the effort, would rendezvous with Hoke at Garysburg, N. C. Both were seasoned, battle-tested units from Robert Rodes' Second Corps division—the 43rd North

(Library of Congress)

Brigadier General Montgomery Corse

Carolina of Junius Daniel's Brigade and the 21st Georgia of George Doles' command.

The selection of the 21st Georgia was not made at random; the hand of the brash young Hoke could be detected in this as well. He had personally commanded this unit before it was transferred to Doles and had made an appeal to the secretary of war in Richmond to have it accompany him to North Carolina. His forcefulness was persuasive. The news that it was going on detached service was broken to these soldiers by Hoke himself, who used the occasion to begin creating his ruse. One Georgian recalled:

> *He came in person to the regiment and told us of what he had done, and said he was going to give us a fine time in his native state catching deserters. He complimented us on the many valorous deeds we had performed, and said we needed recreation, and he was going to take us where we could get it. He knew almost every man in the regiment by name, and the*

*men all adored him, and loud, lusty cheers rent the air when
we found that we were off for a frolic with "Our Bob." But,
alas, the culmination!*[39]

While there were few units in the army that could match the
fighting record of the 21st Georgia—a regiment that had been through
the Valley Campaign with Stonewall Jackson, the Seven Days,
Sharpsburg and Chancellorsville—Hoke was well aware of the fric-
tion among its officers. The conflict centered around the conduct of
its handsome, 34-year-old colonel, John T. Mercer.

Another West Pointer, Mercer, from Palmyra, Georgia, had seven
years' experience in the old army, from garrison duty at Jefferson
Barracks, Missouri, to frontier service in New Mexico and California
as a lieutenant with the First Dragoons. Despite his background, he
remained stuck in grade as a colonel while many juniors in the Confederate army passed him by. The reason was all too apparent to
those around him. He "would have attained high rank," said one of
his captains, "had it not been for booze, the bane of the old army."[40]

Just before the Battle of Gaines's Mill, Mercer was actually removed from command and placed under arrest for intoxication. At
Malvern Hill a few days later, Mercer begged for "a chance to re-
deem my reputation" and was restored but in the midst of that en-
gagement suffered from "nervous prostration" and had to relinquish
control of the unit.[41] Despite his woeful performance during the Seven
Days, Mercer managed to keep his imbibing under enough restraint
subsequently to win plaudits in dispatches on innumerable occasions
and gain Lee's confidence to the degree that he hoped to be recommended for promotion. But it never came.

While willing to excuse his drinking, his officers never forgave
him for an incident that occurred just before First Manassas. During a torrential downpour, Mercer had ordered the regiment to strike
its tents. At the time there were a large number of men suffering
from measles. One of Mercer's captains, an eminent physician named
T. C. Glover, asked the colonel not to leave the sick men uncovered
in the rain. One member of the unit recalled that:

*Colonel Mercer refused to listen to him, and peremptorily
ordered the tents down. Captain Glover refused to obey the
order so far as his company's sick were concerned, and was
placed in arrest. The command of the company devolved on
the first lieutenant, who obeyed the order, struck the tents and
left about twenty men with measles lying in the rain. Almost
all the other company officers of the regiment took sides with*

Captain Glover, and the breach thus made was never healed as long as the principals lived."[42]

In selecting the 21st to accompany him, Hoke reasoned that he could handle Mercer, and his weakness for the bottle. What probably meant more to him was another aspect of the tall, blond officer's reputation. While a "tyrant in camp," as one soldier put it, "he was a splendid man in a fight."[43]

After reporting to Pickett, Hoke remained in Petersburg to await the arrival of his brigade while Pickett's troops started ahead. Hoke's own impressions of the ostentatious department commander are unclear, but the situation was awkward. It was Hoke's plan that was being executed, and it was Pickett, totally unfamiliar with the situation in New Bern, who was placed in charge—probably for no other reason than to have a major general present.

Hoke's troops, glad to evacuate their squalid camps on the Rapidan and anticipating the prospect of good foraging in North Carolina, arrived in Petersburg crowded in box cars. With doors spread open to the January cold, the men nonetheless enjoyed the luxury of rail transportation. Hoke greeted them with enthusiasm and was ready to move promptly to Garysburg.

There Hoke had planned to turn his entire expanded brigade over to Mercer, as senior colonel, while he hastened ahead with his staff to Kinston to ready the movement against New Bern. If he anticipated problems with the colonel, he probably did not expect them to appear so quickly. On meeting the "old army" officer at Garysburg, the general detected that Mercer had been drinking. According to Hoke's close friend, Lieutenant Colonel Samuel McDonald Tate of the 6th North Carolina, he "did not wish him to remain in command" of the full force. Because Mercer was the ranking subordinate, Hoke would have to stay on himself to exercise control.[44]

But Mercer's inebriated state was only the first annoyance as Hoke began to see his brilliant plan for wresting New Bern from the Yankees unravel.

(David M. Sherman)

Colonel John T. Mercer

"Rebellion seems to be expensive"

The piercing whistle of the first locomotive of the Atlantic and North Carolina Railroad to arrive in Kinston from New Bern in 1855 not only startled and delighted the inhabitants, but awoke the town from a commercial inertia that had endured for decades. Three years later, when the single-track line was extended west another 40 miles to connect with Goldsboro, the major impediment to the community's development—transportation—had been removed and something of a metamorphosis began.

Shipping had been restricted by the fluctuating depths of the tree-clogged, muddy Neuse. Kinston had been established on a sharp bend of that river in 1740 as a trading post for planters in the area. Roads through the table-flat region were so sandy and loose, as well as circuitous because of the pine bogs that consumed much of the surface, that travel in even a lightly-loaded wagon was tortuously slow and exhausting.

There were only two trains daily to Goldsboro, the day train called "The Shoo Fly" and the night one designated "The Cannon Ball." But even with limited rail service, Kinston's broad, tree-lined and usually deserted streets began to crowd with activity. Whereas an occasional cart loaded with cane creaking along to James Webb's mill to be ground into sorghum was often the only sign of activity, by the end of the decade Kinston's population had tripled to 1,340 citizens—half free, half slaves. A visitor strolling about might observe passengers from the new train depot, brick with a cupola on top and situated in nearly the center of town in deference to its importance, crossing to the St. Charles Hotel for a hot meal during a stopover.

Further down Queen Street could be noticed an even more imposing hostelry operated by one of the four physicians in town, Dr. W. A. J. Pollock, a four-story frame building with an observatory on top from which the guests could see the entire town in miniature below them and trace the meandering of the Neuse. It was known for "an excellent table, the best liquors, plenty of servants, good stables and stable boys, a good supply of ice, and a first-rate well of water in the backyard."[1]

Pollock's was the inn favored by most of the lawyers who had business across the street at the Lenoir County Court House, which stood at the intersection of King and Queen Streets. These two main byways were the only remaining allusions to royalty after the town, in a burst of patriotic spirit during the Revolutionary War period, changed its name from "Kingston" to Kinston.

The brick courthouse, erected in 1845, was an imposing structure in its own right, with its ancient stocks on the green in front offering an amusing curio. Nearby, a huge bell hung suspended between two posts and was rung for special assemblies, though mischievous boys would sometimes sound a false alarm just to create a stir. Out back and gratefully blocked from the view of most bypassers stood an ugly little brick building that the locals regarded as a dungeon, but was simply the county jail long maintained by old Isaiah Wood.

A Methodist and an Episcopal church of modest size were also visible. Crowded between these main buildings were some two dozen white painted wooden structures, housing enterprises ranging from Henry Dunn's printing office to Jasper B. Cummings' tailor shop, a factory for ornamental wood to a grist mill. Indeed, the old town was becoming so busy and prosperous that a man named E. T. Barry ventured to open a studio next to the post office "for the purpose of taking ambertype likenesses, an imperishable picture upon glass by a new process."[2]

The major employer in the town was Dibble & Brother, carriage makers. With the access to new markets that the railroad provided, James and Franklin Dibble's business swelled to the point that 75 workmen were engaged in turning out some 600 buggies and 100 wagons a year. James Webb, a man of many enterprises, also ventured into carriage making but not on the scale of the Dibbles, who had come to Kinston some 20 years before and whose business acumen was much more appreciated by some of the townspeople than their politics, since they were regarded as "Northern men." For a time, they had also operated a steamboat on the Neuse, ferrying both freight and passengers to New Bern, until the railroad abruptly made that activity redundant.

The dominant figure in Kinston as the decade of the 1860s began was John Cobb Washington, as old as the century and a distant relative of President George Washington. His family operated a large foundry, a three story shoe factory and a supporting tannery. They appeared to own much of the real estate in the town, including a group of cottages he provided for the shoemakers he imported from New England that became known locally as "Yankee Row."

While Lenoir County (Le-nore, to those who resided there) had authorized a $50,000 bond issue to help finance the building of the sorely-needed railroad, it was Mr. Washington who had become the prime beneficiary by winning a $340,000 contract to construct the Kinston to Goldsboro segment.

The coming of the war, in the midst of this growth surge, brought further dramatic changes to the town, particularly in terms of commerce. John C. Washington, as might be expected, had been Lenoir County's representative to the secession convention that took North Carolina out of the Union after President Lincoln's call for troops. The young men, as always, could not wait to rush off and join in the fray. They enlisted in such units as the "Lenoir Braves" of the 40th North Carolina Regiment, bound for service at Fort Hatteras (and, for many, a Northern prison camp after its early fall) or the "Dixie Rifles" that would end up in the heavy fighting in Virginia as part of the 27th North Carolina Regiment.

However, to a number of the rustics inhabiting rundown shacks and working near-worthless patches of earth outside of town, raising a few pigs and some Indian corn, this war was unfathomable. They regarded it as none of their business, and from the beginning they resisted being drawn into it. They hid out in the swamps so familiar to them to avoid the conscript officers, who threatened to separate them from the ramshackle homes they had never left nor would.

Early on, the commercial benefits of war began to accrue to Kinston, so much so that the shortage of manpower seemed the only encumbrance to how much money could be made. Mr. Washington obtained an enormous contract to produce shoes for the army. Mr. Webb concentrated on another vital commodity, horse shoes for the cavalry. Mr. Cummings was sewing only uniforms now. The bakery on Queen Street was expanded into a 250 foot long building to produce hard tack. The demand was so great that the proprietor arranged to have Confederate soldiers detailed to him for the work and they could be seen, barefoot with trousers rolled up, standing in a great trough mixing vast quantities of flour, salt and water, with garden hoes to produce the dough for the crackers on which the army subsisted.

Even the hotels benefitted as refugees began crowding in from New Bern and other coastal towns occupied early in the war by the Yankees. These became centers of social activity. A contented member of the 23rd Georgia Regiment found the town "filled with the first young ladies of the state" fleeing the enemy and in need of

protection and companionship, both of which he was all too happy to provide.[3] The visiting wives of officers, also in want of temporary lodging, augmented this lively, transient society.

Drinking places began to appear and multiply as the number of troops in the vicinity grew. This occurred dramatically after a training camp had been established and the Federal occupation of the coastal points made it necessary to set up a barrier around Kinston to protect the railroad and guard against incursions inland by both large units and far-roaming bands of pillagers. Private William F. Loftin wrote home in disgust that he found "nothing but rum shops in Kinston."[4] Another soldier, Samuel P. Lockhart, told his wife of his companions' forays into the community: "A heap of them go without leave or license. They have got three or four of our fellows in jail now for running through the town and getting drunk."[5]

Some of the locals did not know what to make of all the changes the war had brought and appeared to be trying earnestly just to stay out of the way. A correspondent for the Charleston *Courier* who stopped there briefly went away with an image of Kinston as a place where "the women all chew yellow snuff and the men set on the door steps and gape."[6]

When the railroad tracks between Kinston and New Bern were severed after the fall of that port, located just before the point where the Neuse empties into Pamlico Sound, it served psychologically to cut off the threat of imminent attack from that sector. But that sense of the Yankees being a safe distance away was abruptly shattered in December 1862, when an army under Brigadier General John G. Foster suddenly advanced on Kinston at virtually the same time that Ambrose Burnside and the Army of the Potomac were moving against Fredericksburg, Virginia.

The town all but panicked. Businesses were boarded up and residents began to flee with what valuables they could pile on wagons. Those who remained were warned that the Yankees were likely to shell the place. With only a fragile defensive line of Confederates under a gruff, hard-drinking West Pointer named Nathan "Shanks" Evans in front of them by the river to contest a crossing at the bridge, the townspeople huddled in their cellars as Union guns opened fire from the opposite bank. Mrs. Martha Ellen Miller, the wife of a physician, wrote to her brother in her native Boston, of the experience:

> *The cannonading got perfectly furious. Shells flew thick and fast all about; the smell of powder and the shouts of the men were terrible. About two, the same orderly came up and gave us a preemptory order to leave. I told Doctor (he was*

perfectly willing to go) that I could not leave my home. I wept for the first time when he ordered the ponies. Before they came, we knelt down together and I offered up a prayer for protection. My poor husband was so agitated that he could not speak, but wept like a child...the house was shaken to the foundation by the artillery, and the musketry rattled like corn in a popper.[7]

Another lady told of General Evans sending a small spring wagon to convey her to a place of safety with an elderly neighbor. Once out of town, they stopped at what was thought a safe place,

but our conveyance was barely out of sight when a bomb came whizzing over the town and burst a few feet from where I sat. A number of women and children had gathered there before we arrived but that bomb caused such a panic that they all fled as rapidly as possible toward the improvised hospital, Mrs. (Betsy) Green and I creeping along in the rear.[8]

Evans, who one of his officers said "was drunk as usual,"[9] rebuffed one entreaty from Foster to surrender with a remark typical of his manner of speech. "Tell your general to go to hell," he instructed the messenger.[10] But his 3,000 men could not resist for long, and after awhile, Mrs. Miller observed, "the shout went up that our forces were retreating and soon they came pouring through the town," pursued by the Yanks.[11]

A Rebel soldier who had been assigned to burn the bridge with turpentine, one commodity in plentiful supply in that pine region, succeeded only in setting himself ablaze. His burning corpse was skirted by the bluecoats as they rushed over the span and into the streets.

It had been a tough march over from New Bern along an exhausting sandy road for the Federal force. There had been frequent halts to clear felled trees placed as barriers by the Confederates along the way and a number of annoying skirmishes. "Our impressions of North Carolina have not been rendered more favorable by a more thorough acquaintance," Corporal Zeuas T. Haines of the 44th Massachusetts noted. "Much of the territory we traversed is dead, uninteresting level, thinly populated in times of peace, and almost depopulated by the war."[12]

The few rustics they encountered struck the New Englanders as a peculiar lot. "We saw here for the first time women and children practicing the disgusting habit of snuff dipping," remembered Samuel H. Putnam of the 25th Massachusetts Volunteers. "A small stick was dipped into a snuff box and the end is then rubbed over the

teeth and gums, talking while the operation is going on, the stick protruding from the mouth."[13] And after an encounter with pickets in front of Kinston, Corporal Haines recalled:

> *We saw one dead rebel stretched upon a piazza as we passed a house on our right, and marvelled at the stolid indifference of two or three white women who sat near the corpse and gazed at us as though nothing unusual had happened.*
>
> *At one point the column was confronted by a spunky secesh female who, with a heavy wooden rake, stood guard over her winter's store of sweet potatoes. Her eye flashed defiance, but so long as she stood upon the defensive no molestation was offered her. When, however, she concluded to change her tactics, and slapped a cavalry officer in the face, gone were her sweet potatoes and other stores in the twinkling of an eye.*[14]

Following the fight with "Shanks" Evans' men outside Kinston, it fell to Putnam's unit to bury some of the dead Rebels. He noted of the incident:

> *Shallow trenches, not much over two feet deep were dug, and side by side the dead were placed therein, their faces covered, and as carefully as possible the earth was hastily thrown over them, and the order given to fall in. This may seem hard— as one of our boys expressed it, "It's kind o' rough, ain't it fellers?" But there was no other way—nothing else could be done under the circumstances; so we marched on and left them in their—is the next word GLORY?*[15]

David L. Day, a member of the same detail, recalled how "the boys did not take very kindly to this burying business, as they were in a hurry to get into town and secure their share of the spoils, but the job had to be done, and they went about it with a will."[16]

After crossing the bridge into town, Corporal Haines observed:

> *...as we passed through the streets upon our first entrance we found many bales of cotton piled up and set on fire. The Kinston rebels no doubt thought we were dying to get possession of their precious staple. Near the depot, a great pile of corn was also on fire, and afforded a splendid bivouac blaze for some of our troops. A few Union people we found here. One lady hospitably entertained some of the officers and afforded interesting information of the enemy's hopes and discomfiture. They confidently expected to hold the place, but left with great precipitancy, strewing the way with clothing, equipment, guns, etc.*[17]

Almost as soon as they had gained control of the town, the Union soldiers began to loot. Samuel Putnam of the 25th Massachusetts had a somewhat more refined way of putting it. He and his chums, he said, simply "went visiting to look over the property and see what we could find."[18] Mrs. Miller, one victim of the plundering, said "at Delia's (a Vermont woman living in Kinston at the time) they took every article of bed clothing, knives and forks, sugar, honey, preserves, table cloths—in fact, everything." She added, "I heard the spoons rattling in one man's pocket and made him give them up and brought them home with me. I felt more like crying then than I had for the day. The shells and balls were ruth warfare, but this plundering a Northern lady's house was more than I could endure."[19]

When the cannonading ended and she was able to return, a daughter of George McRae, operator of the St. Charles Hotel, found that:

...everything had been taken from the hotel that was worth having. Mother...was in terror because my father would express his opinion of the conduct of the Yankees in such forcible language that they resented it by threatening his life on the spot. One officer drew his sword and dared him to utter another word. Father was so furious because he had just put up meat to be used at the hotel and he had accumulated other necessary articles of food, all of which the Yankees either took away or destroyed before his eyes. Besides they had set fire to Coleman's drug store near the hotel and the flames were threatening the St. Charles.

The Yankee soldiers feasted and revelled at our house all night and next morning the back yard was strewn with the remains of dead animals. I remember seeing a hog with one ham missing, but the poor beast had been dismembered not butchered, and the Yankees ate the ham before the animal had time to cool, if indeed it was dead. The feathers of geese and chicks were all around and parts of sheep with the wool unremoved. The sight was revolting and I cannot express what my soul endured.[20]

Mrs. Miller noted that "Mr. C... (a tailor, a Southerner, but refused to furnish materials or to make a secession flag when the rebellion broke out) stayed with us till 3 o'clock, was then told by an orderly that the town was on fire, and he must leave. He did so, and what was the result? Everything was taken." In concluding her dreadful experience, she wrote: "Oh, my dear friends, you know not the horrors and ravages of war. I hope you never may. The town is ruined, the people crushed. Rebellion seems to be expensive."[21]

For his unit's part in the sacking, Private Day of the 25th Massachusetts confessed that as soon as they went into bivouac, they:

> *...commenced the destruction of fence and old buildings for fires, and after supper parties went up town to look over the prize, and late in the evening began to return bringing in their plunder. One party had been very successful; they came in hauling an express wagon loaded with tobacco, cigars, applejack, scuppernong wine, pigs, etc. Of course, a divident was struck and all that wanted had a share in the tobacco and cigars, with a drink or two of the wine and applejack. This was a pretty good Sunday's job.*[22]

Samuel Putnam had the impression that "this seemed to be a great wine country, and we got hold of some very good wine and applejack or apple brandy, a more plebian drink but quite passable."[23] In his view, "there was, strictly speaking, no pillaging—no houses were interfered with that were inhabited—but there is no doubt about it, chickens, pigs and such like did suffer some."[24]

With most of its members suffering the consequences of their dissipation, Foster's army moved on unsteadily to Goldsboro before withdrawing to the coast and the stunned Kinstonians numbly approached the task of restoring normalcy. First the injured had to be given attention. A hospital was set up in the Methodist church and another at Nichol's store where one resident said she saw "hundreds of hands and feet already severed from their bodies standing in buckets...and heard men pleading with the surgeons to save their limbs."[25]

Gradually businesses began to function again. Mr. Cummings soon was producing Confederate uniforms in quantity with the help of a number of soldiers detailed to him for the work.

Once the Yankees were a safe distance away, officers of the Confederate navy floated down to Kinston a ram they had under construction 17 miles upriver in order to have it plated at James Webb's foundry. For months, the incomplete ironclad was a fixture at the bank while Mr. Webb laid a temporary track from his shop to the river to transport the heavy parts for the vessel which had been fitted with an engine removed from an Atlantic and North Carolina Railroad locomotive. Eventually, the authorities hoped, when it was finally ready, the ram would clear the waterway of Union gunboats. Officially, the craft was designated the CSS *Neuse*, but so much difficulty was encountered in its construction that the idle crew privately referred to it as the "Neuse-ance."

A new enterprise flourished in Kinston, one about which the community did not boast—prostitution. Some said it began with a group of camp followers who General Foster had permitted to accompany his force for morale promotion, and who had elected to remain behind when the bluecoats departed. Town authorities saw to it that the fancy ladies confined their trade to a section on the outskirts of town called Sugar Hill, so named because that was where the privies were dumped. But even in this ambiance, the brothels grew steadily in number into a red light district that was to become legendary. The Confederate soldiers and the civilians were apparently not bothered by the girls' readiness to service customers from either army or accept both greenbacks and Confederate script for their efforts.

Besides the traditional diseases associated with this work, smallpox was also affecting the area. A long line of tents was set up by the river outside of town for sufferers, along with another hospital in an open field and a third in an old house on Heritage Street. All were carefully avoided by the townspeople.

It was into this bewildering, contradictory atmosphere of fervent patriotism and indifference, fearlessness and timidity, feverish activity and idleness, youthful vitality and dreadful illness, gentility and debauchery, stability and transience, that in the last week of January 1864, the cars of the Atlantic and North Carolina Railroad began delivering the ragged regiments of George Pickett's makeshift little army.

No one in town could imagine what in blazes was going on as trainload after trainload of soldiers was emptied at the depot. The men congested the streets as they disembarked and stood about in mobs leaning on their muskets and resting their blanket rolls and haversacks on the sandy ground, waiting for their shouting officers to herd them off to camp sites. The guests at the St. Charles filled the windows and entrance of the hotel to gape at all this sudden activity. Frightened horses, long confined in the cars, shied and resisted as grooms struggled to guide them down planks, while artillerymen cursed under the strain of unloading their field pieces and caissons with heavy ropes. Unauthorized scouts soon took advantage of the halts and delays to venture forth from the depot and snoop about the streets and note for their messmates such attractions as the ample number of whiskey dispensers at this new location.

The soldiers' presence in Kinston was puzzling. Entreaties to officers brought some references to rounding up deserters in the area. But the size of the force and the presence of artillery made that unlikely. And there were few deserters about Kinston, except for a bunch from old John Nethercutt's battalion of partisan rangers who had skedaddled a few months ago when that unit had been joined with the 66th North Carolina Regiment, and had headed for Virginia. Those men were just home guard, and had been promised that they were never to leave the Kinston area. When further pressed, the officers let out that there was talk of another Federal advance inland that their longhaired, dandyish General Pickett was supposed to prevent.

The people of Kinston had a pretty good idea of what was going on in the area, and there had been no inkling that another incursion was being mounted. There had been some trouble with the "buffaloes," those low-class North Carolinians that the Yanks had recruited who went around in herds like bison, ravaged homes in the area and terrified the occupants. Still, the townspeople suspected that there was something else afoot, something that the army was not disposed to discuss.

After the experience of Foster's attack the previous year—and the many burned and abandoned businesses in town served as a daily reminder of that visit—the inhabitants did not rejoice to have such a huge body of soldiers overwhelm them, even if they were Confederate. Soldiers were soldiers, and if not kept under tight control, there was bound to be trouble. And there was enough already with all the brawling that occurred at the drinking places, and out on Sugar Hill. Many residents had already left town in search of more tranquil environs. Midshipman R. H. Bacot, waiting with the impatience of youth for the CSS *Neuse* to be finished, and apparently not one given to carousing, complained in a letter home: "I find it exceedingly dull here as the town is completely deserted by all of its respectable inhabitants."[26]

John H. Peebles, a longtime Kinston merchant who had joined the migration, wrote from Goldsboro by way of explanation for his change of locale:

> *I deemed it imprudent to remain in Lenoir longer as every once in a while the Negroes were leaving for the Yankees and the impression is that they will come to Kinston this winter and there will be a general stampede of the Negroes.*
>
> *I am advising my particular friends to remove them up the country and many of them are doing so—the blood & thunder*

fellows have long since done so, they you know, were to whip the Yankees in no time, but the first booming of the cannon on our coast they took fright, and left the true men to protect the country.[27]

A member of the 14th Virginia Infantry, who arrived in town ahead of his unit and had to kill some time there on his own, concluded in a letter home that "whoever it was who spoke of 'leaving this world & going to New Jersey' had certainly never been to Kinston." The soldier further said that he, "had to wander about the town all day & never did I have such a dull time. Though a tolerably large place, everything was closed up & I couldn't help thinking that it was Sunday instead of Monday. It was court day & there were about 20 persons on the street—which I was informed was quite a crowd. I haven't been in since the reg't got into camp, & don't care ever to see the place again."[28]

Even the community's leading citizen, John Cobb Washington, was rarely seen about anymore, though when there, he made a point of entertaining General Pickett at his richly-appointed residence. Tailor Jasper Cummings showed his hospitality by fitting young Brig. Gen. Hoke for a new uniform right after his arrival.

It was obvious that Pickett did not wish to linger in Kinston (or let his presence in such force be known) for no sooner had the last trainload of his troops arrived than the camps that crowded every undeveloped patch around the town were struck and the regiments formed to march.

Save for his personal staff, Pickett hardly recognized the men under his command. Hoke and his officers were total strangers. His own units were but slightly more familiar; the colonels and other field officers were new to their positions and still not trusted, and the veterans in the ranks wore a dispirited look of stoic resignation since Gettysburg. Even their unweathered banners were strange to Pickett, almost all the old battle-torn standards having been lost on Cemetery Ridge.

This would be Pickett's first taste of independent command, with a force larger than he had ever led. Away from his mentor and protector Longstreet, who was off in Tennessee with the First Corps, Pickett was totally on his own.

Following his instructions to the letter, Pickett began his movement against New Bern on the morning of Saturday, January 30. He sent forth as an advance element the experienced Brig. Gen. Seth Barton with Armistead's old brigade and that of Kemper, three regi-

ments of Matt Ransom's North Carolina brigade, eight rifled pieces, six brass Napoleons and 600 cavalrymen.

The units represented more than half of Pickett's total strength and deservedly so, because Barton would have the primary role in the operation. He was to move south, cross the Trent River, and follow it to New Bern where that river converges with the Neuse to empty into the sea. Barton was to use his cavalry to cut the railroad and telegraph lines and prevent reinforcements from reaching the Union garrison from Morehead City. Then he was to seize the bridge over the river, rush his infantry and artillery across, and take the Federal works in the rear. With the numbers at Barton's disposal, these steps appeared manageable enough.

Later in the day, Pickett sent off two Virginia regiments to report to 24-year-old Colonel James Dearing, still another West Pointer. In command of a battery and 300 cavalry and, with the added infantrymen, Dearing was to launch an attack from the north side of the Neuse on Fort Anderson at Barrington's Ferry.

On Sunday morning, Pickett's amphibious element of more than 100 marines under Commander John Taylor Wood, began to descend the Neuse aboard a flotilla of 14 cutters for an attack to be made that night on the Union gunboats thought to be in the river by New Bern. Once the vessels were captured, it was planned to turn their own guns on the Federal fortifications. A brazen scheme, yet with the Yankee sailors lulled by months of inaction and boredom, a surprise attack by a small band of boarders just might work.

Finally, Pickett that evening started out with Hoke's augmented brigade, three regiments of Corse's and two of Brig. Gen. Thomas L. Clingman's, as well as 10 pieces of artillery, leaving Kinston uncommonly quiet and barren of men in uniform. In the complex scheme, this last element under the major general's direct observation, was to divert and draw the enemy's attention from Barton as he surged into town from across the Trent.

Nothing in his orders stipulated just where Pickett should position himself. It is curious, then, why he should have chosen not to accompany Barton when his was so clearly the pivotal role in the attack. Was George playing the old army game of covering his rear end, in the event the plan went wrong?

Just as Foster's Union infantrymen had discovered a year before in moving in the opposite direction, the Confederates found the road between Kinston and New Bern brutally punishing. Infantryman Benjamin H. Sims with the 17th Virginia remembered it as "the sandiest road I ever saw" and insisted that he "never saw more sore

feet and broken down men before" than were lining the 30 mile route to New Bern.[29]

As they labored down the Dover Road, Hoke's men tried to keep their approach undetected by arresting any local citizen they encountered who as much as happened to notice the column in motion. The chance of being given away, however, was remote in that sparsely populated region. Said one artilleryman trailing along with Stribling's battery, "we had to travel by night for a large portion of the way over a most desolated country, there being four houses on the road in 20 miles traveling & only two of them inhabited." What the gunner found fascinating on the trek was the local practice of "barking" pines to facilitate burning:

> *The scene was quite picturesque as on one side of the road you might see the tall pines which had been barked for about six or seven feet from the bottom lighted up by the rosin burning on the other side and looking like an immense church yard or an army of ghosts. The trees that were set on fire seemed to be fiery giants stretching their arms out to each other in mutual greeting. The rosin which is collected on the trunks of the trees by means of this barking renders it very easy for the fire to consume them.[30]*

Barton's movement, almost parallel to Hoke's though separated by the twin rivers and spongy pine bog in between, was made memorable by a fast-spreading grass fire that someone had carelessly set off during a halt and which seriously threatened the force's ammunition caissons.

Captain Charles W. Squires of the Washington Artillery had dropped in exhaustion after helping to drag the unit's heavy guns through the consuming sand when the blaze erupted. It was "with only the greatest difficulty did we beat out the flames and save our ammunition," the captain recalled but in the effort, he lamented, "my pants, boots and gloves were burnt up, and the voracious flames did not spare the tail of my great coat. I had no other clothes...the cold winds were searching and pitiless."[31]

Disarrayed and nervous with fatigue, the various elements struggled to the positions from which, on Monday morning, they were to launch a simultaneous attack. Almost immediately, everything that possibly could go wrong did. Barton sent out his cavalry repeatedly to cut the railroad and the telegraph lines to Morehead City to isolate the New Bern garrison but his riders kept returning to report that they had run into resistance and were unsuccessful.

Dearing found Fort Anderson too strong to risk an attack and decided to wait for assistance. Judging the earthworks and blockhouses he encountered guarding the approaches to the bridge at New Bern too formidable, Barton also hesitated and sent couriers to Pickett for further orders. Commander Wood had launched his skiffs and after drifting silently downriver for miles the raiders discovered the Federal gunboats gone and no vessels to board, no guns to turn.

With this string of negative reports coming in—all related to some extent with faulty reconnaissance for indeed the whole plan was based largely on information Hoke had gathered weeks before—Pickett could sense another humiliation developing rather than the redeeming victory he coveted. Accompanying Hoke's men, he could see trouble developing in their sector as well.

Hoke—quickly embraced by the units added to his command, and proclaimed by one member of the 21st Georgia as "the best office[r] we every was under"—had hoped to surprise the Union pickets before they could take up the bridge over narrow but deep Batchelder's Creek in front of the New Bern defenses.[32] But to the anger of the approaching Confederates, the bluecoats managed to rip up the planking just moments before they arrived at the other end of the span. A mere squad of Yankees had brought the advance to an embarrassing halt. With a haughty feeling of omnipotence, the fast-moving pickets observed the regiments of Rebels they had forced helplessly idle on the far side of the creek. Meanwhile, word was rushed back of the enemy's approach and the long roll abruptly began to summon defenders into the Federal works.

Trying to press on as rapidly as possible, Hoke ordered some trees felled along the bank. Two regiments under the hard-drinking senior colonel, John T. Mercer, used the horizontal trunks as walkways to cross the creek single-file while the lone bridge was being hastily restored. All during the time that he was forced to witness this clumsy river crossing, a fuming George Pickett could hear the rumbling of trains approaching from New Bern on the Atlantic and North Carolina tracks, carrying reinforcements to the forward lines. And he could only wonder where Barton was, and why he did not attack.

Hoke, his quick mind always working, attempted to intercept one of those coughing trains bringing troops to his front with the bold intention "to place my men upon it and go into New Bern."[33] It would have been a spectacular entrance, to deposit a regiment smack in the interior of the Federal lines, but that scheme also went awry. The train sped away just as Hoke and his men were rushing into position to board it at a bend.

Under heavy fire, the young brigadier finally was able to advance to within a mile of the town. There he awaited the sound of Barton's guns from the opposite side of the Trent. After finding a vantage point, Hoke could see through his glasses two trains chugging into town from Morehead City, "which proved clearly that Barton had not reached the point of destination."[34]

Pickett grew more and more furious at Barton, not only for his failure to sever the railroad line, but also for his inability to advance his infantry into the town, though he had no real idea of whether the obstacles in front of his subaltern were surmountable or not. In exasperation, he sent his aide de camp, Captain Robert A. Bright, wading across the Trent to urge Barton to either advance or rejoin Pickett with his force for a combined frontal attack.

The harassed Barton, with a fresh memory of defeat and not ready to take any risks, exploded on the staff officer that "he had been entirely misinformed as to the strength of the place." Stating that the position was far too strong to chance an attack, Barton directed the young captain to inform Pickett that "he had made no advance and did not intend to."[35]

When one Union gunboat, the *Underwriter*, did appear unexpectedly on the river, Commander Wood wasted no time in surrounding it with his small boats. The raiders were about to seize the vessel when its commander fired his revolver into her powder magazine and blew her up, thus depriving Pickett's force of even that meager capture. With that obstacle out of the way, however, many of Barton's own men thought that he should have attempted an attack on the town. Artilleryman Squires was one of them: "General Barton was much censured by the officers for not pushing his advantage and taking New Bern with the stores known to be there," he related, adding that, "I believe the city could have been taken."[36]

Less enthusiastic about such an effort was infantryman John L. Stuart, who wrote: "I tell you I was relieved the most you ever saw for we thought we would have to charge the city but our Generals found it was too strongly fortified."[37]

The cautious Barton saw myriad difficulties in trying to cross the Trent and rejoin Pickett. The alternate plan for an attack en masse had to be dropped as well. With all element of surprise gone and "trains coming in constantly night and day from Morehead City," the commanding general took stock of his situation and "deemed it prudent, after consultation with my officers, to withdraw, which we did at our leisure."[38]

To the men in the ranks, however, "at our leasure" actually meant having to slog their way back to Kinston in a heavy, relentless rain. Most had not even fired a shot and had no idea why the operation was being so abruptly abandoned after their long trek. The road soon became "one vast mudhole about the consistency of batter and about shoe-mouth deep as a general thing, with frequent places of much greater depth," noted one soldier.[39]

"The roads were fearful," Captain Squires recalled. "All along the route trees of fat pine were set on fire. The flames gave us light but greatly endangered our ammunition."[40] Then, the rumor spread that a Federal force was in pursuit and the men were urged to double-quick. "It was a picturesque scene," observed another officer, "this rush of muddy men along an illuminated muddy road."[41]

With each slowly traversed mile, Pickett's anger grew. If he had viewed the operation as a fresh opportunity to balance his defeat at Gettysburg, he could not have been more disappointed. Here he was, with a vastly superior force, retreating in disorder from New Bern after only a feeble effort at wresting it from long Union occupation. His casualties, in this, the largest operation he had ever personally directed, were "about 45 killed and wounded."[42]

When he got around to writing his official report to General Lee, Pickett smugly stated that he had been "afraid from the first" that the battle plan handed him was faulty, "as there were too many contingencies." Yet Pickett had done little to improve coordination among the various elements so that the plan would work. When he said "unfortunately there was no cooperation," he overlooked the fact that ensuring coordination was his primary responsibility. And when he said that he had found "we were making the attack single-handed" he made himself sound as if he were in charge of Hoke's sector only and not the overall operation.[43]

Young Hoke, for his part, seemed a bit too anxious to minimize the miscarriage of his grand scheme, concluding in his own report that "the troops do not look upon our campaign as a failure, as the real object was not known to them...."[44] Odd reasoning.

Pickett may have already begun to frame his official explanation in his mind as he rode along in the rain, his horse struggling awkwardly in the consuming mud and tossing him about roughly. His men saw nothing dashing about their commander now with his drenched curls hanging lankly and unflatteringly about his head and, by his expression, knew better than to approach him. To what extent the frustration and disappointment of this abortive campaign influenced Pickett's subsequent behavior is a matter of conjecture.

The capture of New Bern and its vast stores was Pickett's primary mission, but he had one other objective: to seize a band of North Carolina deserters known to be serving with the Union garrison as members of what was being referred to locally as the 2nd Loyal North Carolina Regiment. Several scouts had been sent forward to locate the defectors' whereabouts. Among them was a young captain of the 8th Georgia Cavalry, John G. Smith, who would never forget his harrowing experience. Stationed in the Kinston area for several months, Captain Smith had recently enjoyed the companionship of his wife, who stayed with other visiting spouses at the lively Dunn residence.

At the time he was summoned to undertake the special scouting mission, the captain and his troop had ventured to a point within ten miles of New Bern and had come upon an odd sight in that desolate region. They discovered "one of the old time, ante-bellum residences, on a magnificent plantation that seemed not to have been raided by either army, as it seemed to have everything on it that was good to eat, so the few days we were there, we had things bountiful, and paid for them in Confederate money."

The captain made his camp in a grove near the river. While there, savoring the comforts of this storybook location, a dispatch arrived which directed him to report immediately to his commanding officer. This was no small request. He was needed to slip into New Bern as a spy to ascertain the whereabouts and strength of the block houses and forts protecting the town. "I was also charged," he recalled, "to pay special attention to the location of the camp of Confederate deserters also asked to get the number in camp."

That evening a scout escorted the captain to a point on the picket line where he could pass undetected. The scout then took his horse back while Smith—disguised in a U.S. Army uniform that would be enough to hang him if he were caught—began to stroll about the darkened streets of the coastal town as nonchalantly as possible.

Smith carefully noted where troops appeared to be deployed and any indications of their state of readiness. When someone pointed out to him in conversation the house where the Union commandant was residing, he reasoned that this might be the very place to secure maps and other information and brazenly went up on the porch. Hearing nothing from inside, Smith entered the unlit house through an unlocked door. From somewhere in the darkness, an authoritative voice demanded to know who was there. Smith blurted out a fictitious name. As the surprised colonel continued his verbal as-

sault, a side door opened and a young lady entered with a lighted candle to illuminate the room for the waiting commandant. It gave off just enough light for Smith to recognize the holder as someone he had recently met at an affair in Kinston. He had, in fact, spent much of the evening dancing with her (and with more delight than a young husband should ever admit to). On seeing him, Miss Puss Dunn exclaimed to her instant regret:

"Why Captain Smith!"

"I had my hand on my pistol, and the young lady threw the candle to the floor, and it went out, while I kept the colonel covered, and made my escape to the porch," the exposed spy related.

Running in the rain through the dark, deserted streets, Smith reached the Union picket line and "by the flashes of lightning could see that the sentinel on the line before me was sitting down, so I at once concluded he was asleep." Making the shaken sentinel his prisoner, Smith got the man to guide him to a point where he was to rendezvous with Rebel units when the advance began and deliver his information.

> On my return to camp, I had turned gray, and was otherwise so badly disfigured in my Yankee uniform that neither my body servant nor Dr. Johnson, the surgeon of the battalion, knew me for several hours. I had turned gray, but when, or where I do not know, but my candid opinion is that it occurred after I had been recognized by my young lady friend in the colonel's room.

Yet in his brief career as a spy, the young officer had been successful in securing much of the information he was sent to gather. The next day he had recuperated enough to escort Colonel Mercer and his Georgians, after they finally managed to get across Batchelder's Creek, directly to the training ground of the North Carolinians in blue that the Confederate authorities were so anxious to get their hands on. "There were several hundred of them in camp here, and they were as worthless a set as ever trod the soil of North Carolina, and their actions thoroughly proved the saying that a man who won't fight for his home and family won't fight anywhere," he bitterly recalled. "We flushed them like a covey of birds, and captured 45 of the number, others fleeing to the block houses, none of them offering any resistance."[45]

But a member of Mercer's command did not remember it being quite that easy to bag them and was reminded of how Hoke had misled them about their mission during his initial visit to the regiment back on the Rapidan. In his version, they had found "the de-

serters General Hoke had spoken of, but he failed to tell us when we were so jubilant over the prospect of the fun we were going to have in capturing them that they were in the Yankee army and that we would have to fight like blue blazes to get them. Oh no, he didn't tell us that."[46]

After hoisting a white flag over one of the block houses when he saw the size of the Confederate force closing in on it, a Union officer warned some other members of the 2nd North Carolina serving under him that they could not expect to be treated as prisoners of war and both allowed and advised them to slip off, before the capitulation, and save their necks. This was not the sort of protection these men felt they had been promised by the Federal government but they seized the opportunity nevertheless. The fleeing group was seeking the safety of the familiar swamps when a scouting party of the 30th Virginia intercepted the turncoats and herded them back to join the other prisoners.

While the Confederate officers regarded with contempt all these Southerners who had been low enough to join the Union ranks, they were primarily interested in determining which ones had deserted their side before doing so. In this, they received some unexpected help from a few of the prisoners themselves, men anxious to improve their positions with their captors by becoming informers.

Major Walter Harrison, Pickett's inspector general, described these accusers as "wretches who were well known, not only as deserters, but as the worst of marauders and depredators upon the borders after their desertion." Once caught, they "had no idea of suffering alone." One was a sergeant, according to the staff officer, who "had his company roster in his pocket and actually designated the deserters upon it by name, and picked them out for the provost marshall."

As much as the Confederates looked upon the informers with disdain, their assistance was proving invaluable. Harrison was convinced that "but for the dastardly and miserable denunciations of their own comrades in guilt" a majority of the deserters would not have been detected.[47]

Almost all the men being pointed out and then pounced upon and dragged off for special treatment—conspicuous in their new and incriminating dark blue jackets and pale blue trousers—apparently had been members of a home guard unit known as "Nethercutt's Battalion." Two, however, were recognized as having belonged to a regular Confederate army regiment, the 10th North Carolina. The former were insisting they were not deserters because they had never

been members of the Rebel army as such. Higher authority would have to resolve that distinction and decide what to do with these men, now growing apprehensive and increasingly uneasy. For the time being, their captors decided to keep them separated from the other prisoners and they were placed in the charge of the provost guard.

One man who had acquired a pretty good view of what was in store for the prisoners was a 46-year-old private of the 10th North Carolina named Blunt King. In his earlier days, King was a dutiful and impressive soldier. He had gone to Mexico with the 1st North Carolina Volunteers, and had even been promoted to sergeant for his service. But his interest in this present conflict was minimal. In fact, he was hardly recognizable as a soldier both because of his age and the fact that he often chose to wear "citizen's clothes." He much preferred taking it easy playing cards with the boys than all that drilling and saluting, and this New Bern trip was just too much hard work for a middle-aged man. And especially with his having been detailed to ferry heavy wooden pontoons about, loading and unloading them on and off railroad cars and wagons, and not ever seeing them put to any sensible use.

It was when they were about four miles from New Bern after the fuss around Batchelder's Creek that Blunt noticed that fancy general from Virginia, Pickett, talking to one of his officers and decided to lend an ear and maybe try to find out something of what was going on. But he couldn't make much sense of what Pickett was jabbering about. All he could understand was Pickett saying "that every God-damned man who didn't do his duty, or deserted, ought to be shot or hung."

King thought no more about it until on the way back to Kinston when the army camped overnight at Dover. There, he saw some of the Yankee prisoners who had been taken being questioned around a fire not far from the large wall tent that General Pickett occupied. Curious, Blunt mosied over to take in what was going on. Thinking that two of the fellows looked familiar, his lieutenant, H. M. Whitehead, confirmed for him that these two men, Joe Haskett and David Jones, were men formerly from his company. They had even fought at Fort Macon with them before having deserted. But they were now in Yankee outfits, and some of the men were saying that they had been taken while serving with one of those new regiments the Yanks were recruiting around New Bern—the 2nd North Carolina Infantry, U.S.A.

Despite the circumstances, Blunt King felt he should acknowledge his former mess-mates. He strolled up to the guarded men and casually called out, "Good evening, boys," and they replied, "Good evening, Mr. King," with understandably little enthusiasm.

Then King and his lieutenant sat down on a log near the fire. In a moment, the flap of the commanding general's tent was thrown open and Pickett emerged, trailed by Hoke and Corse. Pickett came up within a few feet of the hapless captives, looked them over, then took Lieutenant Whitehead aside and asked him about them. King heard Whitehead say that they had belonged to his company of the 10th North Carolina. Pickett then returned to the prisoners and demanded sharply, "What are you doing here? Where have you been?"

They muttered something King could not discern, but what Pickett roared next was plain: "God damn you, I reckon you will hardly ever go back there again, you damned rascals. I'll have you shot, and all other damned rascals who desert."

Accepting the hopelessness of his situation, Jones responded defiantly that he "did not care a damn whether they shot him then, or what they did with him." Pickett ordered the prisoners away from his tent in disgust, and as they were being led away, he turned to his two generals and said, "We'll have to have a court-martial on these fellows pretty soon, and after some are shot the rest will stop deserting." Corse responded with, "The sooner the better."

Whitehead nudged King with his elbow and said, "You hear what they are saying?" Shortly thereafter, the officer and the graying private got up and strode away from the glow of the fire into the gloom wondering, no doubt, what would develop next.[48]

Chapter Three

"An awful cold, bad day"

When the bedraggled force again congested the streets of Kinston en route to camp sites on the outskirts of town, the inhabitants could hardly believe that these exhausted, mud-sullied, downcast men were the same soldiers they had seen arrive less than a week before.

It was soon apparent there was something strange going on that seemed to be preoccupying and angering the officers they confronted as much as the failure to take New Bern and the great cache of provisions all had expected to find there. The citizens watched quizzically as some two dozen sullen Union prisoners were hustled into the Lenoir County Court House, while the infantrymen and horse-drawn batteries continued to move in slow procession past the brick building and out of town. If he had taken the time away from his anvil to observe, the blacksmith Bryan McCullum might have seen his own brother-in-law, William O. Haddock, among the prisoners. A number of people would have recognized the deformed shape of Elijah Kellum and wondered what medical officer had accepted that old wreck, the butt of many jokes, for military duty.

A bit later, Isaiah Wood, the county jailer for as long as anyone could remember, was told that his facility was being commandeered. The blue-uniformed prisoners filed across from the court house and were shoved roughly inside. Wood had never seen it so crowded, even on pay nights at Dibbles and nights when some of the soldiers got too liquored up in town.

The next day appeared to pass uneventfully enough except for a meeting of Confederate officials at the court house, congregating there with armed guards in front to keep everyone out. Going on inside was a court martial for the two former members of the 10th North Carolina who had been captured—Joe Haskett and David Jones— only the first of a series of military trials that would take place there.

The very next morning, the Kinstonians observed more peculiar things. In that big sandy patch of open ground behind the jail, shirt-sleeved soldiers were laboriously sawing and hammering together a platform. Thinking it to be a reviewing stand of some sort, onlookers speculated and went on about their business. While this odd activity was going on, a Rebel captain approached O. S. Dewey, the

post quartermaster in Kinston, and requisitioned some rope. There wasn't any. He was sent to scavenge at the Confederate navy gunboat under construction down at the river.

Blunt King was sitting playing cards, as usual, on one of his pontoons at the railroad depot and waiting for a train to arrive to take the boats back to Goldsboro when an officer approached. Captain Adams from General Hoke's staff found what he, too, was looking for — some lengths of rope. He turned to the card players and asked: "Who can tie a good hangman's knot?"

Some of the boys looked to King as a man handy with rope. Suspecting what was going on after his experience on the Dover road, King muttered under his breath that "if General Pickett wanted any hanging done he had better do it himself."

"What's that you say?" the captain demanded. Seeing that he was headed for trouble, King revised his remark to, "I could beat any man playing seven up." King was ordered over to the place where, it was now apparent, a gallows was being built. Before shuffling off indifferently to his assignment, however, Blunt had ascertained the identity of the officer who had directed him but not because of the nature of the task.

"I was vexed at being ordered on this duty, as I was playing cards at the time," he would later grouse.[1]

Rapidly, talk spread through town of what was going on in their midst. Kinstonians began to gather in shocked fascination about the jail as two of the blue-coated soldiers crowded inside were extracted and roughly assisted by guards to climb atop a wagon waiting in front. They were joined by an army chaplain, hampered in his ascent by having to hold on at the same time to his precious Bible.

As the open wagon escorted by a ragged provost guard creaked along toward the rough platform, jostling the passengers when the loose sand surrounding the stage was encountered, a procession of townspeople trailed along like mourners following a hearse. All were anxious for an explanation from the army authorities of what this was all about.

When King arrived, he saw they were his old friends Joe Haskett and David Jones on the wagon, stopped next to the scaffold with the strikingly handsome minister. The man of God was the Reverend John Paris, chaplain of the 54th North Carolina who was attending the condemned only "at the instance of Brig. Gen. Hoke."

In his brief time with the two illiterate soldiers, Mr. Paris found "they were the most unfeeling and hardened men I have ever encountered. They had been raised up in ignorance and vice. They manifested but little, if any, concern about eternity." It shocked the

minister to see how the pair "marched to the gallows with apparent indifference" and to notice how Jones, "though quite a young man, never shed a tear." To his last minutes with them, the chaplain said the men insisted "that the Yankees compelled them to take the oath and enlist" in their service.[2]

Before Blunt King could fulfill his expert role and adjust the ropes around the necks of the two men (and return to his card game) military ritual had to be observed. The entire brigades of Hoke and Barton had been ordered out to witness the punishment and they struggled like a procession of tottering drunken men over the loose sand to form a gray square around the scaffold dominating the flat field. A 21-year-old lieutenant from Lincolnton, N.C., ironically named John G. Justice, read as loudly as he could from a flapping sheet of paper the charges against the men — desertion and taking up arms for the enemy. He also read the execution order issued by the department commander, Maj. Gen. George E. Pickett, upon his approval of the findings and sentences imposed by the court martial he had appointed.

Many of the high ranking officers were there to see justice done, easily distinguishable in that assemblage of tatterdemalions by their gold-embroidered kepis and tunics of gray, their high riding boots and fine mounts. Among them, looking suitably stern and solemn, were a number who had received their training at the U.S. Military Academy. They had themselves once sworn a solemn oath of allegiance to the same flag these men had ultimately embraced. Some said that Pickett himself, class of '46 and a regular U.S. Army captain, was there, though an aide insisted he had already left the scene. The disfavored Seth Barton, class of '49, who also had been a captain in the regular army, was present. Also attending was Colonel Mercer, whose West Point diploma dated 1854 was signed by Robert E. Lee as superintendent of the academy and whose lieutenant's commission in the U.S. Army bore the signature of Jefferson Davis, as U.S. secretary of war. Perhaps even young Colonel Dearing, who had left the academy in 1861 when the war began and in whom the motto "duty, honor, country" was most recently inculcated, was there.

Did any of these officers sense a parallel between their own course and the vows of loyalty they had taken and these men standing on the scaffold? Outwardly, they could maintain that they, as officers, were free to join in what Washington officially had decreed a rebellion because they had formally resigned their commissions, though many in the North would insist that a simple letter to the adjutant general's office was not enough to merit absolution from their obli-

gations. There was a certain analogousness in their situations and what might be their own fate if their cause failed.

With the formalities disposed of, the condemned men's heads were covered with rough corn sacks in lieu of the customary black hoods that could not be procured. As the traps were sprung on the crude mechanism that had been erected in the sand, the builders, new to such work, hoped nervously that their devices would function properly and that the agony of the condemned men would not be prolonged. They performed to grim perfection and in an instant the pair was limply suspended. The troops, long accustomed to seeing bodies torn apart by grape and canister, gasped open-mouthed at the sight of bound men having to surrender to death so unstrugglingly.

As the last of the subdued witnesses—for whom the exercise was intended as a dramatic warning lest they be entertaining any thought themselves of crossing the lines—filed slowly and uncertainly back to their camps, someone noticed the lifeless bodies being cut down and Blunt King busily slicing the shiny buttons off the blue tunics.[3] That night, Corporal Sidney J. Richardson of the 21st Georgia alluded to the executions of Joseph Haskett and David Jones as a postscript to a letter to his parents in Lumpkin, Ga.:

> *Oh! I fergotton (sic) to tell you I saw two Yankees hung to day, they derseted (sic) our army and jiyned (sic) the Yankey army and our men taken them prisoners they was North Carolinians. I did not maned (sic) to see them hung. Well I will tell you more about it next time."*[4]

Southern press reaction to the abortive effort to retake New Bern was unusually prompt and the editorial comments decidedly unfavorable toward Pickett, which added to his discomfiture. Opined the Wilmington, N. C., *Daily Journal* on February 6: "Last year we besieged Washington for several weeks and came away without accomplishing anything. Now we have witnessed a repetition of the same thing with regard to New Bern, only it has not taken so long to do nothing."

Three days later, William Holden's *Standard* in Raleigh cuttingly predicted that history would judge Pickett "unequal to his opportunities." In the Yankee papers, Pickett was further ridiculed. A headline on page one of the New York *Times* on February 21 jeered GENERAL PICKETT'S FIASCO and asked sarcastically:

...was it probable that the large importation of forces from Virginia, the gathering of seamen from Savannah and the James for the purpose of taking New Bern was to end in such utter failure? We had reason to expect that a more serious effort would be made by the Confederate army....

This whole movement must have had a political as well as a military object. It was to check, at least, the growing disaffection in North Carolina with the Confederate Government, so called. Its political effect, however, may be worse than single failure for this abortive effort of the army.

Though intended to discourage desertion, the operation, by its feebleness, had only led to further discouragement in the ranks and as many men apparently abandoned Pickett's force as were recovered at Batchelder's Creek. In another New York *Times* story headed REBEL DESERTERS, it was reported on February 15 that :

...about two dozen Confederate deserters who came into our lines at New Bern arrived here from that place yesterday afternoon and were marched to the Park and set at liberty. They then dispersed, either to pass the night at the Soldier's Home, 52 Howard St., or wherever curiosity or good will might extend them an invitation. They wore slouch hats and butternut clothes, with fragments of carpets or blankets pendant as cloaks. They belonged to Georgia and North Carolina regiments and enlarged vehemently upon the discontent prevailing in their respective regiments at the prolongation of the war and its indifferent prospects for Confederate success. The men were all Americans and showed intelligence and politeness. They were very anxious to go to work, and during the present demand for labor, will undoubtedly find it.

Union officers dutifully monitored the Secesh papers for valuable military intelligence and rarely were they disappointed by the correspondents who paid little attention to security concerns in their reportage. But it was a small item that appeared in a Richmond newspaper on February 8 that suddenly aroused the ire of Maj. Gen. John J. Peck at the once-more unthreatened headquarters at New Bern of the Army and Department of North Carolina. Peck was himself a West Pointer, class of '43, and a Mexican War veteran. He had left the army in 1853 to launch a successful career in banking and railroading in his native upstate New York and had returned to active duty at the outbreak of the Civil War. While experienced enough not to be overimpressed with the veracity of reports on mili-

(Library of Congress)

Major General John J. Peck

tary operations as given to and disseminated by the press, Peck, as the commander of a large number of black troops, was clearly alarmed by this particular account.

After reading the communique, the 43-year-old Union general addressed a letter to his Confederate counterpart, Pickett, who had been his adversary during the Suffolk campaign as well. Dated February 11, the dispatch to be delivered on the next flag of truce boat began:

I have the honor to inclose a slip cut from the Richmond Examiner of February 8, 1864. It is styled "The advance on New Bern," and appears to have been extracted from the Pe-

tersburg Register, a paper published in the city where your head-quarters are located.

Your attention is particularly invited to that paragraph which states that "Colonel (H. M.) Shaw was shot dead by a negro soldier from the other side of the river which he was spanning with a pontoon bridge, and that the negro was watched and followed, taken and hanged after the action at Thomasville."

The Government of the United States has wisely seen fit to enlist many thousand colored soldiers to aid in putting down the revolution, and has placed them on the same foot in all respects to her white troops. The orders of the President on that subject are so just, full, and clear, that I inclose a copy for your information.

The angry Federal commander then went on to quote Lincoln to Pickett (having most assuredly no idea of their former close association so many years before) with the key phrase in the chief executive's order stating "that for every soldier of the United States killed in violation of the law of war a rebel soldier shall be executed."

Peck's closing comment was: "Believing that this atrocity has been perpetrated without your knowledge, and that you will take prompt steps to disavow this violation of the usages of war and to bring the offenders to justice, I shall refrain from executing a rebel soldier until I learn your action in the premises."[5]

He soon got an idea of the hardness of the man he was up against — as well as his racial attitudes — when an equally irate Pickett responded:

I have the honor to state in reply that the paragraph from a newspaper inclosed therein is not only without foundation in fact but so ridiculous that I should scarcely have supposed it worthy of consideration; but I would respectfully inform you that had I caught any negro who had killed officer, soldier, or citizen of the Confederate States I should have caused him to be immediately executed.

As to the threat of a retaliatory execution, Pickett declared that, "I have in my hands and subject to my orders, captured in the recent operations in this department some 450 officers and men of the U.S. Army, and for every man you hang I will hang 10 of the U. S. Army."[6] While waiting for the reply to his initial message to Pickett, General Peck had, perhaps in anticipation of trouble of a different sort, written a second dispatch to the Confederate leader, one which he would later deeply regret:

> *General: I have the honor to inclose a list of 53 soldiers of the U. S. Government who are supposed to have fallen into your hands on your late hasty retreat from before New Bern. They are loyal and true North Carolinians and duly enlisted in the Second North Carolina Infantry. I ask for them the same treatment in all respects as you will mete out to other prisoners of war. I am, respectfully, your obedient servant, etc."[7]*

Before he could hear from Pickett on this score, another newspaper clipping was handed to Peck that confirmed his fears were well based. On February 8, the Fayetteville *Observer* reported under a headline that read TRAITORS EXECUTED a brief item stating that, "Among the prisoners captured by our forces near New Bern were several deserters from our army. We learn by an officer just from the spot that two of these have already been executed and others are undergoing trial." In sending the newspaper report on to Pickett, Peck stated the hope that it "will prove to be unfounded" but warned:

> *Having reported this matter to high authority, I am instructed to notify you that if the members of the North Carolina regiment who have been captured are not treated as prisoners of war the strictest retaliation will be enforced. Two colonels, 2 lieutenant colonels, 2 majors and 2 captains are held at Fort Monroe as hostages for their safety. These officers have not been placed in close custody because the authorities do not believe that any harm is intended by you to the members of the Second North Carolina Regiment."[8]*

But events were fast outpacing the exchange of correspondence, what with slowness of passing pouches and the added problem of locating Pickett whose whereabouts were frequently changing. By the time Peck's appeals had reached the Virginian, he had already acted again, to the horror of the residents of Kinston and to many of his own men.

The Kinston tribunal had continued to meet in private, admitting no outside counsel and leaving behind no records of its proceedings other than the findings required to carry out the executions. The gallows dominating the field back behind the brick court house, though shunned and avoided by the townspeople, remained standing while the courtroom activities determined whether it would have any further utility.

Even the identity of the members of the court remained a carefully protected secret. The officers apparently were willing to accept the assignment and provide the result the department commander desired, yet they were not ready to have their names associated with the action, either for fear of retribution from the Federal authorities or shame for having had a hand in it.

Pickett would go only as far as to say, by way of identifying his court, that it was made up of "officers from North Carolina, Georgia and Virginia."[9] His inspector general, Major Walter Harrison, was a bit more expansive, revealing that the board was composed of "seven of the most intelligent and humane officers in the service—four field officers and three captains."[10] But even he declined to cite their names.

Having disposed of the two deserters from the 10th North Carolina, the court was then ready to deal with Nethercutt's men, deciding for manageability or security to try them in two groups. There were 13 defendants in the first set brought before the board, all looking, despite their obviously new blue uniforms, unkempt and disheveled from days of miserably close confinement.

Major Harrison apparently attended the trials for he had much to say about how the defendants were treated by the court, however reluctant he was to name their judges, and may well have been Pickett's personal representative. He brought to the assignment neither a professional soldier's nor a lawyer's view. Something of a hell raiser in his early youth, the 30-year-old Harrison had attended the Virginia Military Institute but because of his poor performance there (including such antics as riding his horse into the cadets' dormitory) had been denied a degree. Subsequently, he pursued a business career in New York City and returned from there to Richmond when the war erupted. He soon came into contact with Pickett and managed to find a place on his staff.

The prisoners were, by Harrison's report, "tried by the rules of United States courts-martial and under the articles of war, identical in effect with those of the United States." And, accordingly, "most of them could have no chance." Nevertheless, "wherever there could be any mitigation of the offense, it was allowed by the court in their favor, and every defense urged for them," he averred.

The judge advocate, in his view, was a man "of talent and kindness of heart" and saw to it that "these unfortunate and misguided wretches could have suffered nothing for want of justice or mercy."[11] Though Harrison would not, someone else identified the man as a Captain Richardson of the 8th Georgia Cavalry.[12]

Were the defendants really given every consideration? Bryan McCullum, for one, hardly thought so based on his experience. When he learned that his brother-in-law, William O. Haddock, was being brought over for trial in the group of 13, McCullum left his livery stable and showed up with a local lawyer he had retained to represent the defendant. He found to his chagrin that "the court-martial would not admit him."[13]

And if he had been permitted to appear before the court, how might this small-town barrister have defended his client in such a venue? Certainly, he might well have sought a postponement to allow a minimal amount of time to research and devise a suitable response to a charge that carried the threat of capital punishment. If in its anxiety to satisfy the commanding general and quickly set examples to discourage further desertions, the court insisted on immediate disposition of the case, the lawyer could have demanded at least that he be given the opportunity to summon and question witnesses.

If he had been permitted to spend any time with his client, the attorney would probably have found Haddock little different from the other defendants, men who seemed to have poverty, ignorance and political indifference in common. Mainly small farmers, they appeared to have only one interest in the civil strife swirling about them in that coastal region and that was to minimize their personal involvement. They would do whatever they had to in order to avoid being taken away from their run-down homes, evading or embracing one side or the other as circumstances demanded. It would be difficult to argue a deep sense of patriotism or loyalty to the U. S. government on behalf of such a lot.

The lawyer might have tried to make the technical point that these men could not be considered deserters from the Confederate army because they had originally enlisted in a local unit before it was incorporated in a regular regiment and that they had an oral commitment from their recruiters that they would not be transferred from the vicinity of their homes.

If permitted to do so, the defense counsel might have challenged the very legitimacy of the court. For these men, in the final analysis, were captured in the service of the U. S. government, a government that officially viewed the conflict as a rebellion. Can one be rightly considered a "deserter" for refusing to take further part in an insurrection and re-affirming loyalty to the established government? The contention could have been that if there was treason, it was on the part of the members of the

court, not the defendants. But such an approach would have made an impossible demand on the Confederate authorities to relinquish their claim to belligerent status.

The hard reality was, however, that there was no argument on behalf of these men that could have been successful with this panel. The one prevailing reason that they were on trial at all was that the department commander, George E. Pickett, was convinced that some harsh, dramatic action was necessary in order to put an end to the problem of desertion endemic in that area, and thus maintain his ranks. The officers of the court knew why they were there and what their roles were in this judicial charade and played them out.

If the quality of justice being administered in Kinston may be questioned, its dispensers could at least maintain that the defendants' rights to a speedy trial had been honored. All 13 men had been tried, convicted and sentenced within 15 days of their capture and their executions were to be carried out the very next day after the court's decision had been unhesitatingly approved by Pickett.

Producing testimony against the prisoners was a simple matter for the prosecution because the same sergeant who had pointed out the defendants on his muster roll volunteered to testify against them. "I am happy to say that this fellow's cruel villainy availed him nothing," Major Harrison pointed out. "He was the last one tried by the court, after testifying against his companions, and one of the first hung after his conviction. He had felicitated himself throughout, that his treacherous state's evidence would save him."[14]

The sergeant's name has also been lost with whatever records were kept of the so-called trials. Indeed, the very names of the defendants are passed on in various phonetic spellings which they themselves — illiterate men for the most part — would not be able to say were correct or incorrect.

The tender consideration to which Major Harrison alluded was not apparent in the way the men had been handled at the county jail either before their condemnation or afterward.

Mrs. Celia Jane Brock, who lived four miles outside of Kinston on the Wilmington road, had somehow learned of the incarceration of her husband, John Brock, and walked to town to see him. "He told me that he got only one cracker a day; all the other prisoners said they only got one cracker a day each," she would relate. If she had not undertaken to bring food to the group, Mrs. Brock was convinced that they would have starved.[15]

Mrs. Elizabeth Jones — another in the pathetic assemblage of wives and mothers lingering about town waiting for the brief visits the jailers allowed each day and for the dreadful time of execution — found her husband, Stephen, without even a cot. "I carried bedding to him myself to keep him from lying on the floor," she said.[16]

The only appeal made on behalf of the prisoners came, curiously enough, from the man they were said to have deserted, 40-year-old Lt. Col. John H. Nethercutt from neighboring Jones County. After visiting them in their congested cell, recognizing many by name, Nethercutt went to General Hoke to ask him if they couldn't be spared. Hoke told him that "he could do nothing, as he had an order for their execution."[17]

Seeing to the spiritual needs of such a large company of sinners after sentences had been imposed fairly overwhelmed Chaplain Paris. The minister described the conditions in which he labored:

> *The scene beggars all description. Some of them were comparatively young men; but they had made the fatal mistake; they had only 24 hours to live, and but little preparation had been made for death. Here was a wife to say farewell to a husband forever. Here a mother to take the last look at her ruined son; and then a sister who had come to embrace, for the last time, the brother who had brought disgrace upon the very name she bore, by his treason to his country.*
>
> *I told them they had sinned against their country, and that country would not forgive; but they had also sinned against God, yet God would forgive if they approached him with penitent hearts filled with a godly sorrow for sin, and repose their trust in the atoning blood of Christ... Some of them I hope were prepared for their doom. Others I fear not."[18]*

At some point, the hardly compassionate Colonel Mercer of Georgia was given the news that he was responsible for carrying out the next round of executions as the senior colonel with Hoke's Brigade. Pickett himself had left Kinston and returned to Petersburg.

To what degree Mercer involved himself in the mechanics of carrying out the responsibility is not known. But as a man who at West Point found the study of engineering the most stimulating part of the curriculum, and early on had thought of pursuing a career in civil engineering, the colonel could appreciate that dispatching 13 men in a single day was no small undertaking. For that matter, Mercer probably had never heard of so many soldiers being executed at the same time.

The approach decided upon — with or without Mercer's active participation — was one certain to make a lasting impression on anyone who witnessed the event (and had any thought of deserting the Rebel ranks). A huge scaffold with an extended overhead beam was erected to hang all 13 of the condemned men simultaneously! Sergeant Leonidas Polk happened to notice the preparations for achieving such a feat and mentioned in his letter home that night that "they are erecting additional gallows today upon which will suspend 13 more of these criminals on Monday."[19]

But further help was going to be needed to carry out such a chilling task. Fortuitously for the Confederate soldiers who might otherwise have had to do the hanging, a volunteer appeared on the scene, a strange looking civilian from Raleigh, a tall, heavy, dark-complexioned man with a crossed eye. Afterward, no one could claim to even know his name. But he had agreed to do the work for a fee that would include a rather peculiar bonus. He wanted permission to keep the clothing of the dead men. Apparently seeing nothing macabre about such a request, the Confederate authorities, anxious to delegate the responsibility, assented. A merchant later heard the hangman bragging in his shop about his role in the goings-on and readily admitting that he "would do anything for money."[20]

On the morning of the executions, two of the condemned — brothers John and Joel Brock — were escorted down to the Neuse by George W. Camp, a shopkeeper who was also an ordained Baptist preacher, and were baptized. A soldier of the Fayette Artillery observed that after their immersion in the muddy river the brothers, about six feet tall and almost identically built, "were taken to the jail to change their clothing and from thence to the scaffold."[21]

Someone said there was music being played as the prisoners filed over from the jail and formed a long row on the creaking platform. Chopin's funeral march perhaps, rendered by one of the small, tinny regimental bands and being played in an environment the composer could have only regarded as bizarre. Hoke's Brigade was re-assembled in the traditional hollow square with some other units. Lt. Col. Samuel McD. Tate of the 6th North Carolina thought that his superiors were particularly interested "that these men were executed in presence of Hoke's Brigade as an example to such as might be weak-kneed among the North Carolina soldiers."[22]

Watching two men hang was unnerving enough for the soldiers; the sight of 13 silent young men stoically waiting for death's arrival had turned many of the observers queasy. The mysterious hangman methodically went about his chores — affixing the rough corn sacks over their heads, securing the nooses in place and maybe admiring

in the process the quality of the workmanship that went into their blue jackets. After a roll of drums an officer read aloud the sentences of the court, the formal phrasing seeming irrelevent to what was about to take place. With startling abruptness, the traps were sprung and the ropes stiffened. Left swaying side by side, with heads unnaturally tilted, were the following men:

A. J. Britton	William O. Haddock
John J. Brock	Calvin Huffman
Joel Brock	Stephen Jones
Charles Cuthrell	William Jones
W. C. Daugherty	Jesse Summerlin
John Freeman	Lewis Taylor
Lewis Freeman	

"It was an awful cold, bad day," Captain Smith of the 8th Georgia Cavalry would remember long afterward, "and the sight was an awful one to behold."[23]

A report that got to the Nashville *Times* noted that the deserters "met their fate like men, even the Confederate soldiers were moved to tears at the spectacle." Depressed by the experience, Sergeant Polk acknowledged that, "I am not fond of seeing the execution of fellow men, deserving as they may be of this awful penalty."[24]

The Rev. John Paris.
(N.C. Regiments)

"The scene was truly appalling," said Chaplain Paris of seeing the row of men suspended from the one long beam. But, he reminded himself, "it was as truly the deserters doom. Many of them said 'I never expected to come to such an end as this.' But yet they were deserters, and as such they ought to have expected such a doom."[25]

Mrs. Stephen Jones had been visiting her husband every day for two weeks, offering what encouragement she could in her bewildered state. When hope was exhausted, she said farewell to him in the crowded cell on the morning of the execution and then clustered with the other kinfolk to await their deprivation. When the moment came she admitted turning away, saying, "I could not stand to see it." When it was over, she said, "I carried my husband's body home with me that same day," the manner and the place of interment having become a matter of total indifference to the Confederate officials.[26]

But for most of the men, dishonor did not end with death for the avaricious hangman quickly went to work stripping the lifeless bodies. General Hoke himself was particularly offended by the blue uniforms and may have had a part in the decision to undress the men. When Bryan McCullum, the blacksmith, approached the general for an order to get William Haddock's body, he remembered being asked "if I wanted my wife's brother buried in a Yankee uniform."[27]

The burly McCullum and some friends got to the body with the order just as the executioner was attempting to take the shoes from the feet of Haddock while he lay in his crude coffin. They stepped in and told the ghoulish figure that they had a directive that this body should not be molested which he reluctantly respected.

One new widow going among the corpses laid out by the scaffold noticed that the Brock brothers were still clothed and "the others were partially stripped, except their under-clothes. Some entirely."[28] In general, the remains were given over to whoever claimed them with little attention to record keeping but three of the men, with no kin about, were simply interred in shallow graves under the gallows.

Mrs. Nancy Jones had come twelve miles for her husband, William Jones, and found him in a shameful state with "nothing on but his socks." She could locate no conveyance to bring him home for burial and had to make the long journey back to her farm alone. Several days later, she sent her 15-year-old son and her nephew, who was 17, to recover the body. The boys found it in an old loft under a guard who at first refused to release the decaying cadaver

without authority. Mrs. Jones said bitterly that, "plenty would have been glad to have assisted me, but did not dare to for fear of being called Unionists."[29]

And still it was not finished.

At about the time the hangings of the North Carolinians captured in Union blue were taking place, another group of prisoners was being disposed of by Brig. Gen. Montgomery Corse in a different fashion. Serving as judge and executioner, the Virginia banker presided over a court martial that tried six Confederate deserters captured in the area with arms in their hands and, after they were found guilty, Corse supervised their punishment.

In this instance, the men were to be shot — indicating they were not among those who had actually gone over to the enemy. The condemned were tied to stakes, in a kneeling position, and were all shot to death simultaneously.

The general's son would later write that Corse considered his role in the proceeding the most unpleasant duty of his life. Indeed, the men under him averred that they had never seen a responsibility "bear harder on man than did this duty on General Corse."[30]

The gloominess of Kinston did not help the general recover from the sad scene in which he had figured. He was missing his wife and on March 9 wrote that "your absence at this dull little place gives me the blues extensively." But it was difficult finding accommodations for even a general's spouse. "The same complaint prevails here that exists in Goldsboro," he wrote. "Want of subsistance."

"There is a Mrs. Miller who says she will take us in if we cannot find any other place in the town, but she seems to be so uneasy & indeed averse to do so that I cannot yet make up my mind to bring you from a place where I know you are tolerably comfortable." If he was alluding to the Boston-born Mrs. Miller, her cool attitude might easily be understood, given the way the captured soldiers in blue were being treated.

With their town under the virtual control of the military, the inhabitants groused over the shocking scenes being enacted there but made no formal protests, though many regarded the penalties imposed as unbalanced for the crimes alleged. Those with Union leanings, and there were many, were recognized and tolerated to a degree in the community and would not risk jeopardizing their live-

lihoods, if not their very freedom, by complaining. Merchant Aaron Baer was one who had apparently gone too far in demanding explanations because he suddenly found himself under arrest as a spy. While being escorted to the provost marshal's office, he saw General Hoke on the piazza and attempted to approach him. "Don't you speak to me, you damned son of a bitch," was the greeting he got.[31]

After the executions had been going on for several weeks, and with more likely to come, the scaffold became a familiar, accepted feature on the local scene. "I could see the gallows from my house," said J. H. Dibble, the carriage maker, "but did not go down."[32]

"It was a sort of general hanging down there," Colonel Tate of the 6th North Carolina described of that period. "There were so many executions that I was considerably worried at having to take my men over so often." It was not for fear of a mutiny or riot by the civilians; rather, it was because of the need to traverse "such deep sand" to get into formation on the field, the officer explained.[33]

But the tough going did not appear to discourage the soldiers venturing about the town in other pursuits. In spite of (or perhaps because of) all these ugly hangings taking place, the drinking establishments and the brothels became even more raucous. Sergeant Polk wrote home about this time that "a Lieutenant went to town, got drunk, had a fight, got cut pretty badly, but of course nothing is said. Another higher in rank goes to town gets drunk, falls in the branch, ruins fine clothes...."[34]

Private Henry J. H. Thompson thought it enough, for the sake of discretion, to merely say of the place, "the wimen (sic) in general dress very nice here, but there is some bad houses."[35] Midshipman Bacot, by now a longtime resident who had witnessed the moral decline in the town, complained in disgust that "all the cider was made into apple brandy and the county is flooded with it. It makes me heart sick to see how drunkeness rules throughout our land. One man in Kinston, which is filled with bar rooms, sold $4,500 worth one day!"[36]

Such was the atmosphere that even a public performance of capital punishment had difficulty competing for attention. Said one member of the 43rd North Carolina rather offhandedly of his excursion, "I went down town, but did not go to the hang."[37]

From the time of their arrival in North Carolina, it was apparent that a good many of the Virginia soldiers had taken an intense dislike to both the state and its inhabitants — a feeling that appeared

to be widely reciprocated, which added to the tension growing over the executions. William H. (Buck) Cocke of the 14th Virginia Regiment, Barton's Brigade, wrote his family of the Kinston region:

> *We are among a set of people who are considerably under the influence of Holden & consequently quite disloyal. They profess to hate Virginians & say it is because they have always treated Carolinians so badly in Va. driving them from their doors & refusing to feed them &c, but they can never point out a single case. I think they are beginning to come around a little now as they see we don't care anything for their dislikes & intend to pitch into them if they grow troublesome. One feminine asked some of our men why they couldn't let the N. C. troops stay here & defend their own state — they told her that they had been tried but there wasn't tar enough on their heels to make them stick.*[38]

At another time, in fouler mood, "Buck" professed that "the good for nothing hole is not worth having, if it was only out of the way so as not to interfere with us & I hope as soon as the war is over it will disappear from the face of the earth some dark night."[39]

Artilleryman Hodihah Lincoln Meade of Dearing's Battalion, writing home on one occasion on some fine stock, an increasingly rare commodity, said to his Virginia family:

> *The smoke of the pine wood fires is so dirty that it keeps us washing all the time so you must make some allowance for the untidy appearance of this sheet which I took from the Court Martial sitting on those N. C. deserters.*
>
> *The North Carolinians are a very dirty set & I think are excusably considering the wretched country that they inhabit. The people are rotten to the core on the question of loyalty to the South but I believe it is from ignorance as in this part of the state they seem to be a very ignorant set, with no refinement at all. Tell Lottie not to think that all N. C. troops are like these people....*[40]

The longer the troops stayed in the vicinity, the more out of hand they became, particularly when it came to foraging. James Booker of Seth Barton's 38th Virginia acknowledged:

> *We have got an awful bad name since we have bin here. The soldiers dont like the N. C. nor the N. C. dont like the Va. soldiers. Some of the soldiers does act verry trifling...sometimes they go out and steel potatores and hogs. The Gen. sent an*

order here the other day for the men all to be turned out on the parade ground and then search their houses. They did not find but verry little meat in our Regiment though they found good deal in the 53 Regt.... The man that had the meat in our Regt. has desirted since he was caught in his meanness. I expect he will go to the Yankees...."[41]

One member of the 30th Virginia opined that the basic trouble with the civilian population was that "there had been so many troops here that everything has been swept."[42] As deprivations against private property increased, Corse openly deplored "the lawlessness of the troops" and imposed new restrictions on the men to put an end to the "thieving and plundering" that was going on. Soldiers could not leave their camps without written passes from high-ranking officers and additional camp guards were posted. If the "disgrace and outrages" didn't stop, the general promised sterner measures.[43]

By late February, the county jail was finally emptied of military prisoners and made available to the customary venial sinners. In clearing its docket, the court had shown a degree of mercy by deciding not to execute two drummer boys who had been captured, imprisoning them instead. The court had also concluded there was insufficient evidence that one Clinton Cox had ever accepted service in a Confederate unit (and allowed him to die later in a prisoner of war camp).

But seven more men were to be hanged:

Amos Armyett	William Irving
Lewis Bryan	Elijah Kellum
Mitchell Busick	John Stanley
William J. Hill	

That Elijah Kellum was to be strung up as a deserter seemed almost ludicrous to the local residents because of the man's physical condition. William Huggins of Kinston recalled that Kellum had wanted at one time to become a Confederate soldier and said, "I believe he volunteered in one or two companies but none of them would receive him. He was so deformed and he had no constitution."

Later, "some persons who wished to scare him" told Kellum that he was going to be sent to a conscript camp, something he apparently dreaded because he almost immediately headed toward the Union lines instead. Ultimately, it was evidence of some sort from a

Kinston conscription officer that was deemed ample to convict the feeble defendant of desertion. The unlikely soldier had to drag himself along behind the others to the gallows.[44]

The overtaxed Chaplain Paris again found more need for his spiritual ministrations than time would permit him to provide. "As all of these executions had to take place within 24 hours after the publication of their sentence, I had only that space of time to devote to their religious instruction before they went to the bar of God," he lamented.

With this final group, the reverend probed further, attempting to determine how it had come about that they had decided to go into the Union ranks together — and assisting in his questioning the work of the Confederate authorities who had been trying to establish the same thing. "I suggested to them that they owed to their fellow men one duty, viz: that they should give to me the names of the men who had seduced them to desert and go to the enemy," the chaplain explained of his tactics. "This they readily assented to, and gave me the names of five citizens of Jones County as the authors of their ruin, disgrace and death, which names I took down in writing, and handed it into the general's office, and they will no doubt be properly attended to."

On the scaffold, Amos Armyett, eldest of the group, spoke out when given the courtesy of a few last words and the minister took down his remarks: "I believe my peace is made with God. I did wrong in volunteering after I got to New Bern. I would rather have laid in jail all my life than have done it. I have rendered prayer unto God to forgive my sin."

Mitchell Busick also had something to say. In his case, it sounded like a final plea for leniency. "I went to New Bern and they told me if I did not go into their service I should be taken through the lines and shot," he called out. "I was frightened into it."

Unable to respond to final appeals, his executioners waited expressionlessly for him to finish so that they could complete their distasteful task. Finally, according to the chaplain, the departing group had a joint expression read: "We wish a statement made to the North Carolina troops that we have done wrong and regret it; and warn others not to follow our example."[45]

If serving as a model was to be the entire point of their lives, in this too these forlorn men were doomed to failure, for their deaths appeared to be creating a far different reaction than Pickett desired. He had terrified some North Carolinians who had joined the Federals, true, but the cost of his excessive punishment was to disgust his own men and horrify the civilian population.

An added quality of ghastliness was given the final executions by the bungling of the unfeeling hangman from Raleigh. He had somehow failed to set the knot properly around Amos Armyett's neck. When the trap beneath him was sprung, the noose did not tighten and it was almost 15 minutes before strangulation came to put an end to his twisting and thrashing. While his ordeal went on, witnesses were spared only his tortured facial expression by the rough corn sack covering his head.

The town finally began to react as a body to what was going on. When the last set of men was taken out it was "accompanied to the place of execution by a large convergence of people and a strong military escort," a writer for the New York *Times* learned from a correspondent of the Raleigh *Confederate* after the event. He reported in a dispatch from New Bern that "the multitude was moved to tears and openly denounced the cruel massacre, which is causing desertions from the Confederate service by the wholesale, and creating an indignation which, it is feared, will be uncontrollable."

Further backlash to the executions was evident in the altered attitude of Union soldiers toward Pickett and his men. Reported the *Times'* man in North Carolina: "At the unheard of barbarity, our native troops are exasperated beyond all bounds. They have resolved to take no more prisoners. The difficulties experienced heretofore by the officers to restrain them are, by this barbarous butchery at Kinston, greatly increased."

While Chaplain Paris was able to draw out the names of some individuals who might have influenced Nethercutt's men to leave when the unit was incorporated in a regular regiment, further encouragement had come from the local press. In an obvious reference to Holden's *Standard*, the rival *Weekly Confederate* in Raleigh asked about the deserters in an editorial on Feb. 17:

> *Are they only to blame? They left the service, and assumed that of the enemy, on the plea of some fancied wrong done by our government in the removal of Colonel Nethercutt's command from the outpost service, in which they were engaged in Jones and Onslow counties, into General Martin's, and then ordering them to Wilmington. This slight supposed grievance furnished the excuse for their great crime; but was there no newspaper which, circulating in that section, aggravated to their eyes the injury they complained of? Did no newspaper take also the ground that the government had committed towards them a breach of faith?*

If there were, then that paper exceeded the liberty of the press, to interfere, wantonly and injuriously, with the military movement. That paper instigated the crime, and is responsible for the consequences its teaching has produced. When any person gives counsel which leads immediately to the commission of felony, that person is an accessory before the fact.

If these poor, deluded men have friends or kin — and we know Colonel Nethercutt at least to be their friend so far as to see that they have justice — they ought to search the press; and if it be found that pernicious counsels have led to this deplorable crime and its attending calamity, the blood of these men appeals for justice upon all guilty — the instigator as well as the actor.

The issue of the *Weekly Confederate* probably reached the desk of Major General Peck at Union headquarters in New Bern—with its shocking revelation that more of his men had been executed—at about the same time that George Pickett had gotten around to responding to Peck's appeal that the 2nd North Carolina Regiment captives be treated as regular prisoners of war, the entreaty Peck had appendixed with a list of all the men from that regiment who had been taken. Pickett began by thanking Peck for the list "which you have so kindly furnished me, and which will enable me to bring to justice many who have up to this time escaped their just deserts."

With mounting rage at the insolence of the fellow, Peck read on:

I herewith return you the names of those who have been tried and convicted by court-martial for desertion from the Confederate service and taken with arms in hand, 'duly enlisted in the 2nd North Carolina Infantry, U. S. Army.' They have been duly executed according to law and the custom of war.

Your letter and list will, of course, prevent any mercy being shown any of the remaining number, should proper and just proof be brought of their having deserted the Confederate colors, many of these men pleading in extenuation that they have been forced into the ranks of the Federal Government.

Extending to you my thanks for your opportune list.[46]

Peck made no attempt to disguise his anger or sense of outrage in the response he immediately sent Pickett to his disclosures, and he showed himself a man adept enough with the pen to fully convey his feelings:

General: February 13 I had the honor to address you in respect to 53 North Carolinians who had fallen into your hands in your late operations about New Bern. As they were truly loyal men who had duly enlisted in the U. S. Army, I requested the same treatment of them as should be meted out to other prisoners of war. No allusion was made to the question of your right to place these men upon any other footing or to the matter of retaliation.

In your reply of the 17th you inclosed a list of 22 men who have been executed at Kinston, and express the determinaton to punish the balance if proof is found of their desertion from your service.

These men, in common with more than half of the population of the state, were ever loyal to the United States and opposed secession until put down by arbitrary power. A merciless conscription drove them into the service, and for a time compelled the suspense of their real sentiments but was powerless to destroy their love for the Federal Union. With tens of thousands they seized the first opportunity to rush within my lines and resume their former allegiance. Had these men been traitors to the United States at the outburst of the rebellion their claim upon it for protection and sympathy under the circumstances would not have been strong, but in view of their unswerving and unflagging loyalty I cannot doubt that the Government will take immediate steps to redress these outrages upon humanity and to correct such gross violations of usages of civilized warfare. In any event, my duty has been performed, and the blood of these unfortunates will rest upon you and your associates.

In your communication of the 16th you threaten to execute 10 of the officers and soldiers of the U. S. Army for every one of your men, prisoners in my hands, which I shall execute under the orders of the President of the United States, which I inclosed for your information. This announcement, taken in connection with the execution of the North Carolinians and similar proceedings elsewhere, evinces a most extraordinary thirst for life and blood on the part of the Confederate authorities. Such violent and revengeful acts, resorted to as a show of strength, are the best evidences of the weak and crumbling condition of the Confederacy.

This wicked rebellion has now attained that desperate state which history shows is always the shortest of revolutionary

stages. The friends of the Union everywhere truly interpret these signs of madness and recklessness, and are now making one grand rally for the utter overthrow and final extinction of all treason."[47]

Peck could express his outrage to Pickett on a personal level but it was obvious that the even uglier turn the war had taken in Kinston was a matter that had to involve higher authority to bring under control.

❖   ❖   ❖   ❖

The man to whom Peck first turned to acquaint with what was going on in his sector—less the press accounts might have eluded him—was the commander of the Army of the James—Maj. Gen. Benjamin F. Butler. Butler was notorious for his harsh administration of recaptured New Orleans and his order stipulating that any Southern lady who in any way insulted one of his soldiers was to be treated as a woman of the streets.

Short, stout, balding, cock-eyed and outlandishly uniformed with a pair of white spats his trademark, Butler was something of a joke as a military commander by reason both of his appearance and his actions. His genuine abilities were as an opportunistic politician (one who managed to attain his high military rank despite having once been a pro-secession supporter of Jefferson Davis and John C. Breckinridge) and as a first-rate criminal lawyer, renowned before the Massachusetts bar. The conflict in which he was now being drawn over the Rebels' treatment of deserters was more his kind of combat and he plunged in with all his verbal and legal skill.

He approached the problem judiciously, as might be expected. When General Peck had first notified him of what Pickett was contemplating, his response was the lawyer's traditional one of delivering a strong threat. "Send a flag of truce to the Rebel forces, and notify them that if the members of the North Carolina regiment who have been captured are not treated as prisoners of war we shall have to enforce the strictest retaliation, and that I hold two colonels, two lieutenant colonels, two majors, and two captains as hostages for their safety," he instructed his subordinate, Peck. "But say also to General Pickett, that I have refrained from putting these men in close confinement, because I do not believe the story that any harm is intended to the officers and men of the 2nd North Carolina Regiment."[48]

Unfortunately, Bulter's orders arrived in General Peck's hands the very day that Peck learned that Pickett had, indeed, strung up

(Library of Congress)

Major General Benjamin Butler.

22 men and was ready to go after even more. Butler decided it would be politic at this point to apprise the commanding general of the army, Lt. Gen. U. S. Grant, of the situation. He probably had no idea that Grant and Pickett were well-acquainted from West Point days and their service together with the 8th Infantry in Mexico. Nor did he know of the personal fondness they had for one another — despite or perhaps because of the stark differences in their personalities and demeanor. The one was plain and unassertive, the other showy and affected.

In his brief, Butler explained the case as he saw it to Grant:

> *Many of these men were conscripted by the Rebels, all of them were citizens of the United States who owed their alle-*

giance to the Government. *If misguided, they forfeited their allegiance, repented, and returned to it again. They have only done their duty, and in my opinion are to be protected in so doing.*

I do not recognize any right in the rebels to execute a United States soldier because either by force or fraud, or by voluntary enlistments even, he has been once brought into their ranks, and escaped therefrom.

I suppose all the right they can claim as belligerents is to execute one of the deserters from their army, while he holds simply the character of a deserter during the time he has renounced his allegiance, and before he has again claimed that protection, and it has been accorded to him. Thus, by no law of nations and by no belligerent's rights have the rebels any power over him other than to treat him as a prisoner of war if captured.

I would suggest that the Confederate authorities be called upon to say whether they (approve) this act, and that upon their answer such action may be taken as will sustain the dignity of the Government and give a promise to afford protection to its citizens.[48]

Grant may justifiably have been too preoccupied with Lee and the Army of Northern Virginia in the Wilderness to pay too much attention to an incident in distant eastern North Carolina. If anything, his inclination probably was to support his "old army" friend's actions. But Ben Butler's fury was enough to guarantee that this was a matter for which George Pickett would someday be called to account.

Perhaps concerned about the spiritual impact of all they had been forced to witness in Kinston on the members of Hoke's Brigade, Chaplain Paris on Feb. 28 decided to preach a sermon to the assembled unit. That attendance was compulsory, as at the executions, is not likely. His stated purpose in delivering the discourse was "that the eyes of the living might be opened, to view the horrid and ruinous crime and sin of desertion, which had become so prevalent." The handsome young minister with dark, ominous eyes began by referring to the departed as those "unfortunate, yet wicked and deluded men."

"But what was the status of these 22 deserters whose sad end and just fate you witnessed across the river in the old field?" he asked.

Despite having taken an oath of allegiance to the Confederate States of America, he answered himself, "they went boldly, Judas and Arnold-like, made an agreement with the enemies of their country, took an oath of fidelity and allegiance to them and agreed with them for money to take up arms and assist in the unholy and hellish work of the subjugation of the country which was their own, their native land! These men have only met the punishment meted out by all civilized nations for such crimes. To this, all good men, all true men, and all loyal men who love their country, will say, Amen!" The clergyman dwelt at length on the sordid nature of disloyalty, at one point casting the Tories of Colonial days in a role opposite the one they themselves generally looked upon as the position they were taking. "The character of infamy acquired by the Tories of the revolution of 1776 is to this day imputed to their descendants, in a genealogical sense. Disloyalty is a crime that mankind never forget and but seldom forgive; the grave cannot cover it," he warned.

His work with the condemned — 10 of whom he had baptized — convinced him that they had come under evil influence. In fact, he said, "I am fully satisfied that the great amount of desertions from our army are produced by, and are the fruits of a bad, mischievous, restless and dissatisfied, not to say disloyal influence that is at work in the country at home."[50]

When it was over, these men who had already been shown in chilling fashion what they had to fear from their mortal rulers should they ever entertain the thought of leaving the Confederate ranks now had been made aware in fiery and eloquent terms by their chaplain that divine retribution awaited them as well. One can only speculate which approach more impressed them. What is clearer is that all, no doubt, had had enough of this place of ugly death, bitterness and defeat, and were anxious to move on and leave its memory in the dust that their marching columns created.

"Is that man still with this army?"

Probably most incensed by the Kinston executions was a young New York lawyer, Rush C. Hawkins, who had left his practice when the war began (and his beloved and priceless collection of early printing specimens) to organize a regiment of red-pantalooned volunteers that became known as "Hawkins' Zouaves." He was posted on the North Carolina coast in 1862 when he and a Union navy commodore undertook an experiment to recruit loyal local citizens for the U. S. Army.

The first Southerners he had enlisted were from the vicinity of Plymouth and he would recall that, "very few of them were slaveowners, and consequently had little interest in aiding the rebellion. They worked in their fields in groups, with arms near at hand during the day, and at night resorted to the swamps for shelter against conscripting parties of rebel soldiers."

His superior, General Ambrose Burnside, had left the business of whether or not to recruit North Carolinians entirely in Colonel Hawkins' hands and he proceeded cautiously. At a meeting in Plymouth with some 250 possible enlistees, "a free interchange of views in relation to the affairs of the country took place. The matter of great concern with them was, 'What will become of us in case we are captured by the rebels?'"

"We assured them," Hawkins vividly recalled after hearing of the executions, "that the government of the United States would protect them and their families to the last extreme, and that any outrage perpetrated upon them or upon their families would be severely punished."

He felt a special responsibility toward these "humble, uneducated people" and appreciated the difficulty of the step they were taking. "In the Free States," he asserted, "it was an easy matter to be loyal and to talk and act in accordance with ideas of patriotic devotion to duty; but in the South, even to breathe one word in favor of the old Government, or to do a single act which might awake a suspicion that one was not committed body and soul for the success of the rebel cause might bring the inflection of every kind of fiendish insult and outrage."[1]

(Library of Congress)

Colonel Rush C. Hawkins.

To have these people he had encouraged to assert their loyalty treated so brutally by Pickett engendered in Hawkins a hatred for the man that knew no bounds. To him, the Rebel officer became "an inhuman monster"[2] and "a willing butcher."[3] There could be no denying, however, that Pickett's intention to terrify North Carolinians from entering the Union ranks with his public executions soon produced the desired effect. A Union colonel reported that:

> *...the remainder of the 2nd North Carolina volunteers are much excited. I cannot place the least dependence on them for the defense of Beaufort or any other place. They are utterly demoralized and will not fight. Indeed, they are already looking to the swamps for the protection they*

have so far failed of getting from our Government. I can do nothing with them....[4]

Despite their aghast expressions at Pickett's conduct and their threats of retaliation against Confederate prisoners, there really was little action that the Union authorities could take against Pickett himself until the conflict was resolved and they could get their hands on him.

❖　❖　❖　❖

In catching up with his paperwork, Pickett, back in Petersburg, had also undertaken the unpleasant task of compiling his report to General Lee on his abortive New Bern operation. It was a long account for such a brief affair and one reminiscent of his Gettysburg explanation in the readiness with which he was willing to ascribe the failure to others. In a note accompanying the treatise, Pickett informed Lee:

I have but little doubt that had Barton pushed on we might have been successful. I could have only brought four rifled guns into action. Two 10-pounder Parrotts (new guns) were disabled while firing on their ironclads, the first fire disabling the carriages. I am sorry nothing more was done, but the surprise being over, and no co-operation, it would have been a desperate matter to attempt an attack in front. I hope, general, you will understand my reasons for the withdrawal, and remain, as ever, with high respect, your obedient servant.[5]

There was, of course, not a single mention in the report of the prisoners from the 2nd North Carolina that he had taken or how they had been treated. Just how much George Pickett had told his superiors of the vigor with which he was carrying out the announced mission of the expedition — that is, to deal with the problem of desertion — is difficult to ascertain. He had at some point let Samuel Cooper, the adjutant and inspector general, know in a rather casual way that there was a bit of a flap going on regarding his measures (and seemed rather uneasy that he wasn't getting any reinforcing response from Richmond.)

One letter to General Cooper provides an insight to the paradoxical nature of the man whose values were so often difficult to discern. Before even dealing with the Kinston matter, Pickett seems anxious to let Cooper know that he had personally made good a sum of $550 destined for a Federal prisoner of war that was apparently stolen by a courier, a private from the 18th Virginia Regiment, before he deserted to the enemy.

"I send by Captain Bright, my aide-de-camp, the money to Lieutenant Kirby, as it will not do for this officer to lose what was intrusted to my charge, I feeling myself in honor bound," Pickett advised. A matter of honor. "The clothing I have recovered a portion of and send on...." This business disposed of, Pickett got on to the Kinston unpleasantness. "I also inclose, general, copy of letter today received from General Peck. I have not answered it yet. I think the most direct way will be by next flag-of-truce boat.   You will perceive that these men were hung by sentence of general court-martial regularly appointed. If these colonels, lieutenant-colonels, and captains of whom he speaks are deserters from the Federal Army, he can execute them; otherwise it will be murder."

But the following line is the chilling segment of the piece, one in which he indicates his anxiety to make sure he had ample supply to draw on should the Federals wish to match executions with him: "I hope the whole of the prisoners captured in this department will be held at my disposal."[6]

Whether soured by the Kinston executions, the New Bern debacle or both, Richmond officialdom soon turned on Pickett and he found himself suddenly in a peculiar as well as humiliating situation difficult for a man of his vanity to accept.

Enter another figure of some prominence in George Pickett's life. General Braxton Bragg, after a series of calamitous defeats in the West, had convinced the authorities and himself of his unsuitability for field command and, following his resignation as commander of the Army of Tennessee, had been "kicked upstairs." President Davis, whose confidence in the man more than balanced the criticism of his legion of detractors, brought the irascible Bragg back to Richmond, named him his military advisor and made him responsible for strategic planning, a role for which to the surprise of many, he appeared to be most suited. One of his early projects was to work out another operation for Pickett's sizeable force idling about Kinston (and gaining a reputation more for pillaging the property of Confederate deserters in the area than for rounding up the absentees.)

What Bragg had in mind was a sudden attack on the occupied port of Plymouth on the Roanoke River that would utilize the new Confederate ram *Albemarle*. The man Bragg wanted to lead the movement was not Pickett, however, but his energetic junior, Hoke. Had he also come under the young Carolinian's persuasive influence?

While taking his troops from him, Bragg sought to pacify Pickett by saying that the movement was being entrusted to Hoke "so as not to withdraw you from a supervision of your whole department at this critical time."[7]

Left at Petersburg, with virtually only his personal staff about him to command, Pickett endured the waning days of what had been a miserable winter for him. With the troops away, the town was inactive and deserted. There appeared little point in the general even leaving the warmth of the spacious McIlwaine house to go to his bypassed headquarters at the customs building. Sally—expecting their first child—no doubt appreciated having her soldier nearby, what with her parents beyond reach. But there was precious little for the man who was now the senior division commander in Lee's army to do professionally.

When word came that young Hoke had succeeded in wrestling Plymouth from the enemy with its enormous cache of supplies and nearly 3,000 prisoners, Pickett had to mask any jealousy he may have felt and join in the general rejoicing over a sorely-needed victory. President Davis telegraphed Hoke himself to notify him that he was promoted to major general as of the date of the battle and the daring young officer was being mentioned for new undertakings against New Bern and Washington, N. C.

Among the few casualties Hoke had suffered was the loss of Colonel John T. Mercer of the 21st Georgia, who was shot in the head while leading his men with characteristic fearlessness against a redoubt. His death came less than two months after he had been the instrument for dispatching the members of the 2nd North Carolina, U. S. A., to their far more ignominious ends. Rather than the colonel's remains being transported to his native Georgia for burial, the body was removed from Plymouth to Tarboro in Edgecombe County, N. C., where it was interred in the Calvary Episcopal Churchyard in front of the still-mounded grave of Mercer's West Point classmate and distant kinsman, Maj. Gen. William Dorsey Pender, who had died the previous July of a wound suffered at Gettysburg. Another casualty was Corporal Sidney Richardson, the young Georgian who had expressed such indifference to the hanging of deserters.

With the arrival of May came a more crushing blow for Pickett than having been put "on the shelf" — as the career soldiers referred to his type of situation. Pierre Gustave Toutant Beauregard — "Old Bory" — was coming to Petersburg to take over his department and Pickett had orders to report to Hanover Junction and assume command of two of his old brigades. His reign as a

department commander was over — with little by way of accomplishment to show for it. He would have to give up his palatial home and Sally would no longer have — as Pickett joked — "vasals and slaves at her side."[8]

He had hardly begun to evacuate his easy quarters and make plans to relocate Sally at the family's house in Richmond when scouts reported to Pickett that a huge fleet of Yankee transports was moving up the James and was approaching Petersburg. A movement to coincide with the opening of Grant's campaign against Lee on the Rapidan had been expected and now suddenly it was here. And where was Beauregard and what was he to do with one regiment of infantry, an un-uniformed home guard battalion and a few batteries of the Washington Artillery, Pickett did not know.

For a frantic week, Pickett rushed troops about from point to point as soon as they could be procured, trying to ward off Union thrusts against the vital, 22-mile rail link between Petersburg and Richmond. Desperately, he telegraphed the War Department for reinforcements and Beauregard for instructions. During that time, Sally said:

> We women carried the dispatches and cooked the food and took it to the men at the guns. The roar of the cannon and the shriek of shot and shell filled our ears day and night. At traintime we would go to the station and send up cheer after cheer to welcome the train from its short trip out into the country, hoping to blind the Yankees to the fact that it brought in only the half-starved railroad men. During the entire week...my soldier did not sleep, and the only times I saw him were when I carried his bread and soup and coffee out to him.[9]

That Pickett was perhaps taking something else as well to keep him going is indicated in one diary reference during that period that observed, "Pickett is badly dissipated, it is asserted." At the same time, Secretary of War James Seddon was telling Braxton Bragg, "I confess some distrust of Pickett's adequacy to the load upon him."[10]

At any rate, the very day that Beauregard arrived and with the crisis unabated, Pickett reported himself too ill to leave his quarters. Whether it was nervous prostration or some other malady, so long was he expected to be unfit for duty that Beauregard, who had planned in the emergency situation he encountered to keep Pickett with him as a division commander, began making arrangements to replace him. After Beauregard had succeeded finally in bottling up the invasion force under the

bumbling Ben Butler at Bermuda Hundred and Grant and the Army of the Potomac had reached the Richmond-Petersburg defenses, the war settled into a monotonous, dreary siege that was to last for nine months.

When Pickett returned to duty after his breakdown, it was in charge of his reassembled old division which was designated as a mobile reserve for the capital defenses. But the units had lost all cohesion through frequent separation and the ranks were filled with conscripts who seemed to disappear at every opportunity. It was not the same division he had sent against Cemetery Ridge.

To some extent, Pickett's men were spared the harsh, nerve-racking duty of occupying the 37-mile labyrinth of trenches protecting the two cities. They did not have to endure the constant fire of artillery and deadly sharpshooters like most of the other divisions there.

Positioned in front of Bermuda Hundred along what was designated the Howlett Line, Pickett's men had a greater struggle finding enough food in that barren region to keep them together than holding back the Yanks. The usual ration was a pint of corn meal and an ounce or two of bacon a day though one member of the 29th Virginia (a unit that in the last year of the war recorded only one combat fatality, that from a sniper's bullet) said that his mess lived for three days on nothing but frozen turnip tops.[11]

As always, Pickett was able to make himself comfortable. A young lieutenant, new to the army and exposed to Pickett for the first time during the siege, put him down as "a high and a free liver who often declared that to fight like a gentleman a man must eat and drink like a gentleman."[12]

The general conveyed an idea of how he was roughing it through that last long, dreary campaign in a letter to Sally, by relating how he had managed to follow her culinary suggestion that he have an oyster roast with his officers after their conference one night. "I feared we should not have enough oysters," he wrote, but "our old hunter, Gossett, has just brought in a fine large wild turkey, and with that and the three bushels of oysters which your uncle sent I think we can get up a fine supper. Don't you, my marvel of a housekeeper?"[13]

Pickett's lifestyle, particularly as it related to the consumption of spirits, appeared to be accepted, the young officer who had just gotten to know him observed.

"General Lee was a very prudent and abstentious man himself but never censorious touching the mode of life of his inferiors when they discharged the duties assigned them," he noted. "Pickett was a trained soldier and loved fighting."[14]

Physically, the only discomfort the division commander appeared to be enduring was of a somewhat delicate nature. A gentleman farmer in the area trying to arrange a visit for him commented that "the General has been suffering very much for some days with the hemorrhoids and there is no telling when he will be able to ride so far."[15]

It was only shortly after Pickett's return to duty that the news was brought to him by his old overseer Sims that his ancestral home at Turkey Island had been destroyed by Butler. Pickett would have it believed that the act was out of anger over his role in trapping Ben's force at the Bermuda Hundred peninsula but it could as well have been in revenge for the Kinston executions. In relating the development to Sally, George said that the heartbroken foreman had told him that, "they first looted the house and then shelled and burned it, together with the barn and stable." Even a monument in the family graveyard had been overturned. Through the generations, the house had been visited by many of the great men of Virginia history. Curiously, in that Pickett's own life would become so much involved in matters of loyalty, one of the more familiar features of the property was the area where in January 1781 Benedict Arnold had halted on his march to Richmond after leaving the British fleet at Jamestown.[16]

Even if Butler was so embittered at Pickett as to take such measures, the latter was given ample evidence that he still had friends in high places in the Union camp. One month after the loss of his home Sally gave birth to their first child, a son. From across the lines came a dispatch under a flag of truce that said, "We are sending congratulations to you, to the young mother and the young recruit." It closed with the names Grant, Ingalls and Suckley — U. S. Grant, Rufus Ingalls and Dr. George Suckley — three old acquaintances from either Mexico or the Northwest whose friendship would later prove invaluable to him.[17]

That Pickett was not giving his division as much attention as it required during that period of declining fortunes for the Confederacy was evident in a letter General Lee wrote to Lt. Gen. Longstreet, the First Corps commander, outlining in scathing terms the findings of conditions in his command by his inspecting officers. He noted:

In Corse's brigade, the 29th Va. Regt. is reported to be unsoldierly & unmilitary, lax in discipline and loose in military instruction. In the whole brigade the officers & men are indifferently instructed in discipline and drill & the former are said to be inefficient. Commanding officers know but little about the condition of their men & there is a great want of clothing. Prompt measures must be taken to bring inefficient officers before examining boards & get rid of them.

I fear from the reports that the officers of your corps are not sufficiently attentive to the men, and do not keep themselves informed as to their condition. Unless the division & brigade commanders are careful and energetic, nothing can be accomplished. I desire you to correct the evils in Pickett's division above referred to by every means in your power."[18]

The one thing that did continue to hold Pickett's attention was the punishment of deserters. If as much of his energy had been given to improving conditions in his command he might not have had such a major problem on his hands. A dispatch sent by the assistant adjutant general of the First Corps to army headquarters in November 1864 noted:

By direction of Lieutenant General Longstreet I have the honor to state to you for the attention of the commanding general that Major General Pickett reports about 100 men from his command in the guard house charged with the crime of desertion. He accounts for this state of things by the fact that every man sentenced to be shot for desertion in his division for the past two months has been reprieved.

General Lee forwarded the communique to the Secretary of War with the endorsement: "Desertion is increasing in the army notwithstanding all my efforts to stop it. I think a rigid execution of the law is (sic) in the end. The great want in our army is firm discipline."

Not as bloody-minded toward the offenders, who by and large were driven to leave the army not through their own suffering but the plight of their families at home, President Davis reminded the generals: "When deserters are arrested they should be tried, and if the sentences are reviewed and remitted that is not a proper subject for the criticism of a military commander."[19]

Even Sally could not soften her husband's posture concerning those who left his camp, one maintained despite his own history of transferring allegiance. Sally had received a crude letter from a

soldier from her southwest Virginia village who was well-acquainted with her family. The soldier had been condemned to death for desertion and was pleading not as much for his life but the preservation of his good name. He enclosed a letter from his wife, one which had prompted him to go home. It read in part:

> *Christmas is most hear again, and things is worse and worse. I have got my last kalica frock on, and that's patched. Everything me and children's got is patched. Both of them is in bed now covered up with comforters and old pieces of karpet to keep them warm, while I went "long out to try and get some wood for their feet's on the ground and they have got no clothes. neither; and I am not able to cut the wood, and me and the children have broke up all the rails 'round the yard and picked up all the chips there is. We haven't got nothing in the house to eat but a little meal.... I don't want you to stop fighten them yankees till you kill the last one of them, but try and get off and come home and fix us all up some and then you can go back and fight them a heep harder than you ever fought them before. We can't none of us hold out much longer down hear.*

In his letter to Sally, the soldier said he had been denied a furlough but knew that his wife:

> *...would never have written a letter like that unless she was mighty bad off; and I went. I got home allright and seed after them. If I had a staid down thar I would a been a deserter; but I didn't stay — no, I come back, and I ain't one. Seems like luck was against me, though, for just as I was nigh into a half mile of camp that old G— arrested me and I was found guilty and am in the next passel that's got to be took out. When the thing is all done and over I want you, please, marm, to write to the folkes and sorter smooth it down 'bout how it all happened to be. They all remembers you and always asks about you, They sets a heep of store by me, and I don't want them to think nothin' bad of me.... Well, this is the end of the paper, and when you get this 'twill be the end of me, too. Please, marm, don't let none of them down home lose store by me if you can helpt it.*

With heavy heart, Sally approached her husband with the touching letters she had just read. He wasted no time in telling her he could do nothing. As if addressing an aide, the general proclaimed: "Discipline and the exigencies of the service demand a rigid enforcement of military laws."

His words aside, Sally said, "I knew my General's great, generous heart, and I knew that those men would not be shot." The next morning the executions were postponed and three days afterwards an order came from Richmond reprieving the deserters. If she saw her husband's hand in this act of benevolence, she had sadly misread the situation for no one could have been more disappointed by such a decree from higher authority than he.[20]

Despite his fierce attitude on the subject, the desertion problem in Pickett's division — whether due to his inattention or lack of rapport with his men — dwarfed those of other commands. In one ten-day period, 512 men left his ranks while, in that same time frame, another division commander, Maj. Gen. Joseph Kershaw of South Carolina, could report that only 41 of his men were missing.[21]

Pickett's inclination toward capital punishment as the only means of dealing effectively with a problem sometimes extended, it would appear, even beyond the realm of absenteeism or disloyalty. At one point, when he had heard a report that Butler was contemplating a new movement against his lines, Pickett advised Adjutant General Cooper, who by now must have developed an appreciation of Pickett's sanguine nature:

> *Butler's plan, evidently, is to let loose his swarm of blacks upon our ladies and defenseless families, plunder and devastate the country. Against such a warfare there is but one resource — hang at once every one captured from the expedition, and afterwards every one caught who belongs to Butler's department. Let us come to a definite understanding with these heathen at once. Butler cannot be allowed to rule here as he did in New Orleans. His course must be stopped.[22]*

At this point in time, Pickett was as yet unaware of his own vulnerability for the course he himself had taken at Kinston — and particularly from the powerful figure he was now so anxious to challenge. It was in the closing weeks of the war — after he had fallen into relative obscurity while men like John B. Gordon and William Mahone, who had hardly been known in the army at the time of Gettysburg, had risen into prominence — that Pickett was given one last assignment of major importance. And, once more, he would fail to live up to the trust placed in him.

Sheridan's cavalry and infantry under Gen. Gouverneur Warren were making a bold thrust for the vital Southside Railroad at the extreme end of the Confederate lines. Lee rushed Pickett and his division to the scene along with much of his nephew Fitzhugh Lee's

cavalry. Pickett got there in time to block the movement but then was forced to give ground. Showing his alarm, Lee telegraphed Pickett in language sharper than he had ever been known to use. "Hold Five Forks at all hazards," he directed. "Protect road to Ford's Depot and prevent Union forces from striking the Southside Railroad. Regret exceedingly your forced withdrawal, and your inability to hold the advantage you had gained."[23]

This stern rebuke was one that would have shaken the sense of responsibility of another man. On Pickett, the imperative language had only brief impact. The very next morning when an invitation came from cavalry General Tom Rosser to share in the catch he had made in the Nottoway River, Pickett's taste for good food rendered him helpless. The opportunity to attend an old-fashioned shad bake was too tempting; things appeared quiet enough, and Pickett saw no harm in slipping away for just a bit. Stout Fitzhugh Lee was to join in the repast and they rode off together to a rendezvous more than two miles in the rear of the lines. Neither notified anyone of where they were going or when they would return and, what's more, they placed no one else in charge of their units.

By way of explanation for why he felt free to leave his troops, Fitzhugh could only say, "I thought that the movements just then, for the time being were suspended, and we were not expecting any attack that afternoon, so far as I know."[24]

While the three generals enjoyed their delectable fare on the bank of Hatcher's Run, Sheridan launched an all-out assault. The Confederate leaders, out of hearing as well as sight in that heavily-wooded area of what might be developing, learned of the breakthrough only when Federal soldiers suddenly appeared across the stream from them. They tossed aside the skeletal remains of the shad and scrambled for their mounts.

When he reached the front, Pickett could see some dismounted Confederate cavalrymen slowly withdrawing in the face of an advancing Yankee force that threatened to bar his way. "Do hold them back till I can pass to Five Forks," he implored the commander on the scene, Col. Tom Munford. A captain of the 3rd Virginia Cavalry, James Breckenridge, overhearing the entreaty, instantly responded by leading his sharpshooters in a dash toward the enemy. In the effort, the captain was shot dead becoming—in the very last week of the fighting in Virginia—the most direct victim of Pickett's dereliction.[25]

Pickett probably never even saw Captain Breckenridge fall as he leaned over the side of his horse's neck to avoid the enemy's fire and galloped away unscathed. A few minutes later another group of Union

soldiers almost got their hands on the long-haired leader as he tried to rally his woefully scattered command but he answered their demands for his surrender by cursing "damn you" and spurring his horse away once more.

With the collapse of the right flank of the army at Five Forks and the weakening of the rest of the line in an effort to prevent Sheridan from exploiting the breakthrough, the whole defensive system about the capital was about to rupture. General Lee notified the government that the time had come to evacuate. "This is a sad business, colonel," he said to an aide. "It has happened as I told them in Richmond it would happen. The line has been stretched until it is broken."[26]

What was left of Pickett's once-proud division was caught up in the rout at Sayler's Creek on the road to Appomattox. As harried as he was, Lee found time to dictate a brief order releasing Pickett from duty as a supernumerary — in military parlance an officer for whom no command existed that was appropriate to his rank. One diarist, however, suggested a more compelling reason for the extraordinary action:

> *Sad to say General Pickett, Bushrod Johnson and R. (Richard H.) Anderson were relieved from command a few days before the surrender for having been absent from their commands during the fight on the day previous.... In fact, they were all drunk! What a sorrowful thing that men who had won their reputations at the edge of the sword should in a moment of weakness peril it by a gratification of an appetite.*[27]

Although discharged, Pickett continued to tag along, wanting to be around at the rapidly approaching end of the conflict. At some point along the awful trek, Lee happened to notice Pickett riding by himself, and turned to a staff officer and asked disdainfully: "Is that man still with this army?"[28]

After the cease-fire and Lee's meeting with Grant, Pickett was seen with a number of Confederate officers about the tavern at the court house village but unlike Longstreet, Gordon and some others, who had to arrange details of the formal surrender with Union representatives, Pickett had no function to perform. In fact, there was some resentment among the Federal officers, in light of the Kinston executions, that he was being included in the parole the commanding generals had negotiated. As one of Sheridan's officers put it, "There was...not a little chagrin in some quarters that Pickett and other officers of distinction who were deserters from the United States

service at the outbreak of the war should be allowed the same generous terms accorded the others."[29]

What particularly rankled the Union soldiers about Pickett's parole was that they understood, mistakenly, that he had never formally quit their service before joining the Confederacy. According to Charles C. Coffin, a private in the ranks of a Massachusetts regiment:

...many of the officers remembered that General Pickett never had resigned his commission in the United States service, but that he had taken up arms against the country without any scruples of conscience. He was a deserter and a traitor, found in arms. The soldiers remembered that scores of their comrades had been shot or hung for deserting the ranks; the utmost lenience of the government was a long term of imprisonment in a penitentiary or confinement on the Dry Tortugas. Sentinels had been shot for falling asleep while on duty; yet General Pickett and his fellow traitors were, by the terms of the parole, granted an indulgence which was equivalent to a pardon.

It was General Pickett who hung the Union men of North Carolina who had enlisted in the service of the Union but who, under the fortunes of war, had fallen into his hands. In General Pickett's estimation they had committed an unpardonable crime. He considered them as citizens of the Confederacy, and hung them upon the nearest tree. It was cold-blooded murder.

The soldiers idolized Grant as a commander, Coffin asserted, and "they had no objection to his terms with the privates of Lee's army, but there was dissent from including Pickett and Ewell (Richard S.) and other Rebel officers who had been notoriously inhumane to Union soldiers."[30]

As the army dispersed, Pickett — at least for the moment a free man — headed back to Richmond where he had to leave Sally and their baby at the family's town residence at 6th and Leigh streets. The young mother had a harrowing time of it. With the departure of the army, drunken rioting and window-smashing looting ensued. Fires raged with little attempt (or capability existing) to extinguish them. Consumed in the flames were all the wedding presents and personal furnishings the Picketts were keeping in storage at a warehouse, their books, china and piano included.

The terrifying anarchy endured until Federal troops arrived, the first black soldiers Sally had ever encountered. "As I saw their black faces shining through the gloom of the smoke-environed town," she recalled, "I could not help thinking they added the one feature needed...to complete the demoniacal character of the scene."[31]

In the midst of the dreadful disorder, Sally had found herself trapped and unprotected in an empty house, save for her child and her nine-year-old brother, John Theophelas — her servants having all run away — and with the fate of her husband, who was rumored to have been killed at Five Forks, unknown to her.

The day after the most menacing fires had burned themselves out and a degree of calm had returned, Sally heard a sharp rap at her locked door and, with her baby clutched tightly in her arms, she went to answer it, fully expecting that it was to be her turn to have her dwelling violated by felons or soldiers. Instead, she found a carriage stopped in front of her temporary home and a tall, gaunt, sad-faced man in ill-fitting clothes standing before her. In a decidedly Northern accent, he asked: "Is this George Pickett's place?"

"Yes, sir," Sally answered, "but he is not here."

"I know that, ma'am," he replied, "but I just wanted to see the place. I am Abraham Lincoln."

"The President!" Sally gasped.

"No, ma'am; just Abraham Lincoln, George's old friend."

Her infant reached out instantly to the strange-looking man who had been her husband's early benefactor and the president took the child for a moment. Before surrendering him, he muttered, "Tell your father, the rascal, that I forgive him for the sake of that kiss and those bright eyes."

"He turned and went down the steps, talking to himself, and passed out of my sight forever," Sally recalled as he left to resume his brief tour of the captured seat of the Confederacy.[32]

How much of the exchange actually occurred and how much Sally fantasized is, as always with her accounts, difficult to say because, as usual, there was no corroboration. It would seem beyond the realm of imagination, however, to create such a scene if there had been no visit at all from the president.

After waiting anxiously for George's return, Sally said "at last one morning I caught the familiar clatter of the hoofs of his little thoroughbred chestnut which he always rode when he came home, and the sound of his voicing saying: 'Whoa, Lucy, whoa' little girl.'"

Quickly, no doubt, Sally acquainted her husband with Mr. Lincoln's visit, which must have been reassuring to him. After all, a man so well remembered not only by the president but the commanding general of the U. S. Army as well need have no fear of the Federal authorities should anyone be out to make trouble for him. Of far more pressing concern to him, now that the outcome of the war had deprived him of his profession, was finding some means to support his family and restore his ancestral home.

CHAPTER FIVE

"Crimes too heinous to be excused"

Sally Corbell Pickett never quite understood the special relationship that had endured throughout the war among the Union and Confederate officers who had served together in the U. S. Army before the sectional conflict forced them to choose opposing sides. Her husband would refer to it as "this entente cordiale between us old fellows."[1] Her resentment towards all Yankees was still strong to the point of open hostility when quite unexpectedly — only weeks after the surrender — she was thrust in a position of observing George in company with some of his old acquaintances. It was an awkward, confusing situation for the young wife to comprehend.

For the time being, they had decided to reside with her parents at Chuckatuck, some 30 miles from Norfolk, but getting there with their remaining belongings was no simple matter with the railroads in that area still broken up and out of service and they virtually penniless even had the lines been operating. As it happened, Dr. George Suckley, the army surgeon who had served out at Fort Bellingham with Pickett, had paid a call on them in Richmond and was traveling to Norfolk himself on the surgeon-general's steamer the next day. He arranged for the Picketts to accompany him, along with their trunks and horses.

Sally was delighted with the opportunity to return to her home for the first time since her marriage. But she was offended to find that as they were boarding the vessel no salutes were being extended by the Union soldiers and sailors to her husband, still in his gray uniform with lofty rank clearly indicated, only "stares of surprise, of mingled curiosity and hate."

Once under way, the doctor and her husband settled down for an animated exercise in reverie. Sally reported that they reminded each other:

> ...of Texas, and the great annexation strife which had changed the political complexion of the nation away back in what seemed to my youthful view a remote antiquity. They talked of Mexico, and the General recalled reminiscences of the battles in which

he had fought in that wonderful tropical country. They dis-
cussed the wild, free, fresh, novel life of the far-off Pacific coast,
the wealth of the gold mines of California, its luscious and abun-
dant fruits, and the friends they had known there. They talked
of the great Northwest, that was like a mythologic region to me,
of the Chinook Indians, and of San Juan Island and the En-
glish officers who had occupied the island conjointly with the
General. I found myself wondering if it had been a dream, and
there had been no internecine strife.

Sally did not share these memories, of course, and was in no
mood yet for such socializing with anyone dressed in blue, regardless of how kindly and considerate. She was still sulking when the
steamer stopped at City Point and Rufus Ingalls, the army's quartermaster general and another crony from the Northwest, came
aboard for the remainder of the trip down the James. Sensing her
coolness, Ingalls sought to disarm Sally by drawing her aside and
saying, as she recalled:

I don't blame you one bit, little woman — not a damn bit. I
should feel just as terrible about it as you do if I were in your
place. It's all different with Pickett and me, you see. We don't
mind. Why, do you know, child, we have slept under the same
blanket, fought under the same flag, eaten out of the same
messpan, dodged the same bullets, scalped the same Indians,
made love to the same girls — aye, Pickett, it won't do, by Jove,
to tell her all we have done together — no, no — come, shake
hands. I am dreadful sorry we have had this terrible kick-up
in the family, and all this row and bloodshed, but we are all
Americans, damn it, anyhow, and your fellows have been mighty
plucky to hold out as they have. Come, that's a good child;
shake hands.

Rufus tried to extend a token of friendship to the Picketts' son,
as well, a Yankee greenback. When the baby promptly tore it in
half, Sally "caught the pieces and stuck my bonnet-pin through them
until I could paste them together" without daring to mention to the
giver that it was the only money they now had.[2] By journey's end,
Sally's attitude had softened but she was soon to discover that —
especially after the assassination of Lincoln — there were not many
in the North who were as ready as Pickett's old chums to forgive
those who had played leadership roles in the insurrection.

In an effort to re-establish himself in the civilian world, Pickett
sought to obtain official clemency for his participation in "the Rebel-

Major General Rufus Ingalls (seated center) and staff.

lion." Like all officers above the rank of colonel, he had been barred from taking the oath of allegiance that would not only restore his rights of citizenship but enable him to carry on routine business activities. In his application for amnesty, Pickett asserted that had not Virginia seceded:

> *I should not have been in the Confederate army, as no one was more attached to the old service, nor ever stood by, and fought for it with more fidelity, nor could any one have been sadder and more loth to leave it than I, who from my youth had been so devoted to it; and I now am, and have been since the surrender of General Lee (to whose army I belonged,) willing and ready to renew my allegiance as a loyal citizen to the United States Government, and have advised and counseled all men belonging to my division to return to their homes and the peaceful pursuits of life; to take the oath of allegiance, and observe with scrupulous truth its stipulations, and to faithfully obey the laws of their country.*[3]

To get his petition on renewing his "allegiance as a loyal citizen" to the right hands in the U. S. government for consideration, Pickett turned once more to his influential uncle, Andrew Johnston, who had returned to Richmond before the war from Quincy to settle his

deceased father's estate and had remained to establish a lucrative law practice there. Johnston journeyed to Washington — a capital deep in mourning over the assassination of President Lincoln — with the document on Pickett's behalf and looked up his old legal associate from Illinois, the Hon. Orville H. Browning, to solicit his assistance and open doors for him. He could have turned to few men more savvy about the seat of government at that time than Browning, a long-time friend and confidant of Lincoln who had served a term in the U. S. Senate and, upon its expiration in 1863, had stayed in Washington to practice law, and arguing a number of cases before the Supreme Court. He also was actively engaged as a lobbyist for a wide variety of interests, from office-seekers to contractors.

In recording Johnston's visit to him on June 6 regarding Pickett's application — less than two months after Appomattox — Browning noted in his faithfully maintained diary that, "I went with him and had an interview with Genl. Grant upon the subject." Grant, installed now in Washington as commanding general of the army and besieged with problems related to Reconstruction, "spoke in very high terms of Pickett," Browning observed. "Said he ought by all means to make the application, but he did not think his request would be immediately granted — that Pickett had hung some captured Union soldiers in North Carolina on the pretext of them being deserters, and he thought this would be an obstacle to speedy favorable action in his case."[4]

The interview must have impressed Johnston in at least two regards. First, that his friend had developed so much standing that he could readily approach a man of Grant's elevated position. But more important was the revelation that his nephew was in such deep trouble with the Union authorities over his actions at Kinston.

The next day, to the Richmond visitor's further astonishment, no doubt, Browning was able to escort him directly to the executive office of the White House where, after discussing the business of a client — a Cherokee chief, as it happened — with the newly-inaugurated president of the United States, Andrew Johnson, he "also presented to him the application of Genl. George E. Pickett of the Rebel army for a pardon."

President Johnson (who would name Browning his secretary of the interior) "received it kindly — said he was anxious to pursue a policy which would heal the wounds and repair the ravages of war, and bring those who had been in rebellion against the government back to their allegiance, and convert them into peaceable, law abiding citizens; that he had many such applications, and would put this

away with the rest till he could get time to act upon them; but thought he would hold some of the principal leaders in suspense for sometime, etc."[5]

In due course, Pickett's appeal reached the office of Secretary of War Edwin M. Stanton, a man with an abhorrence of all traitors, a loathing intensified with the slaying by Confederate sympathizers of the president he revered. His fanatical feelings showed in the manner in which he ordered the so-called Lincoln conspirators confined before and during their trial, seeing to it that they were kept manacled and (except in the court room) with sacks secured over their heads at all times "for better security against conversation." They were not permitted to remove the bags even to wash their faces.[6]

Another obsession of the portly, energetic Steubenville, Ohio, lawyer was the management of time. Ritualistically, he would devote one hour every morning to meeting with the public in the War Department reception room — and not a second more. For that interval, he would stand irritably at a high writing desk and deal summarily with whatever matters were brought before him. Be they contractors looking for government business, families of imprisoned soldiers or job seekers, the petitioners would have to present their requests in public. Someone who observed the secretary's routine noted how "he would lean his left arm on the desk, settle his spectacles, and wait for people to come and state their business — a peppery little man who looked as though he had not slept well, and as if it would not give him much pain to refuse their most urgent request."[7]

It can only be imagined how much attention a Confederate major general's special pleading received from such a man in his current state of mind. After perhaps pausing once more to rub away with his handkerchief another invisible speck from his well-polished eyeglasses, Stanton scratched across Pickett's appeal: "The Secretary of War reports that Genl. Pickett stands charged with the unlawful hanging of twenty-two citizens of North Carolina, and the case is now under investigation in North Carolina."[8]

The application was thus cast into bureaucratic limbo. Whether Pickett knew at this point that an official investigation was being undertaken against him is not certain. But if notified, he would have no difficulty in concluding who was behind it. Old Ben Butler, out of uniform now, except for the white spats he wore with any ensemble, civilian or military, and now a member of Congress from Massachusetts, had been making the walls of the House chamber

(Library of Congress)

Secretary of War Edwin M. Stanton.

reverberate with his denunciations of Pickett and his calls for federal action against him for the executions. And, with the death of Lincoln, he found his colleagues in a progressively more vengeful mood. Said George McClellan (another "old army" friend of Pickett's) of Ben's objective, what Butler wanted was "to have him tried by a military commission 'organized to convict.'"[9] One reminiscent of the tribunal George had appointed in Kinston perhaps?

Soon things became so hot in Washington that two high-ranking army officers secretly dispatched letters to Pickett by special messenger advising, as Sally recalled, that "in the existing uncertain, incendiary, seditious condition of things, he should absent himself for a while, until calm reflection should take the place of wild impulse, and time bring healing on its wings, and make peace secure."[10]

Sally could never bring herself to acknowledge that there might be something other than Butler's vindictiveness over the wreck of his own military career — as amateurish a bit of play-acting as it

had been — behind her husband's harassment. Nowhere does she ever even allude directly to the Kinston executions, as if they were so inconsequential or so clearly justified an action that there was really no need to make mention of such an unpleasant incident.

To a degree, she felt they were also being victimized by the anger of the nation at the loss of its president, a nation unaware of their own attachment to Mr. Lincoln. In accounting for the arrest of Mrs. Surratt, she said "the first person who could be seized upon was regarded as the proper victim to the national fury" and thought of her husband as being swept up in the same storm.[11]

Only her parents knew that George had decided to leave the country. It was after 10 o'clock at night when he started off on horseback with some circuitous route in mind to get to Canada, where he had friends. Once more the Northern neighbor was serving as a convenient refuge for other Americans in difficulty. Thousands of Northern and Southern young men had fled there during the war to avoid conscription. Pickett had made his way into the Confederacy via Canada and once more he was looking to its boundary line for safety now that the attempt at secession had failed, as were many others involved in the movement.

Before departing, Pickett had worked out with his wife a plan for her to rejoin him in Montreal, but it was a journey that only a person of her age would dare to undertake with a baby not yet a year old. The plan called for her to go to Norfolk the very next day and take the steamboat to Baltimore where she was to stay with an aunt of Pickett's until she received a telegram with the cryptic message "Edward is better." That would mean that he had arrived safely and that she could proceed. If told "there is still danger of contagion," she was to remain in Baltimore. From Baltimore, she was to travel by train to New York City, then by steamer up the Hudson to Albany, proceed overland to Lake Champlain where she would have to board another steamboat north and finally arrive in Montreal by rail—if she were not detected and detained at some point along the exhausting route.

There were no steamers between her home and Norfolk. Her father secured a little oyster boat with a sail and they set off together from their wharf on Chuckatuck Creek, he guiding the craft while Sally held her son with a carpetbag and a basket at her feet. They had hoped to arrive in Norfolk hours before the departure of the Baltimore steamboat but because of a storm they arrived at the levy, drenched and bedraggled, just as the plank was about to be taken in. With understandable trepidation, the father bade a hur-

ried farewell to his daughter and grandchild not knowing if they would ever reach their distant destination or when he might see them again. Suddenly, Sally realized that she was totally on her own for the first time in her life.

At the outset, she had been warned that she must conceal her identity for fear that she might be recognized and held as a hostage for her husband so she assumed identities she, in her nervousness, had difficulty maintaining. On the steamer she had aroused suspicion as a possible fugitive and an undercover federal detective had ordered her detained. However, she managed to persuade the captain to let her off his boat in Baltimore after tearfully appealing to him as a master mason's daughter in distress.

Sally had spent a restorative week in Maryland with George's relations before the wire arrived indicating that it was all right for her to move on to New York by train. She had not enough money for a berth and to travel seated with her baby on her lap. By the time they were on the steamer headed upstate to Albany, both mother and child were totally spent. The absence of his familiar mammy had added to young George's discomfort and he was rapidly growing uncontrollable, to the annoyance of fellow passengers, while Sally struggled in her fatigue to quiet him. Some ladies on board actually became suspicious (it being a period when the nation was obsessed with the idea that it was being engulfed in some vast conspiracy) that the child was not hers and so reported that to the conductor. When Sally could show no proof of her identity, she found herself being removed from the train and placed under arrest and taken before a local magistrate in Albany. He demanded that she telegram for evidence of who she and the child were and where she was taking him. The shaken young mother pleaded that this was not possible but could only offer a feeble explanation of why not.

A kindly elderly couple had decided to stay with her to help her through her ordeal. All during the wait at the court room, George squirmed restlessly in Sally's lap, demanding "the rights of sustenance." The silver-haired woman, her black crepe veil turned back, whispered to Sally as she observed the antics of her child: "Do you nurse your baby?"

"Yes, and he is so hungry — poor little thing."

With that, the woman stood up, leaning on her cane, and called out: "Gentlemen, I have a witness — here, in the child who cannot speak...the child is still nourished from her own body."

The woman gently opened Sally's mantle and,

I, who had never nursed my baby in the presence of even my
most intimate friends, bared my bosom before all those strange
men and women and nursed him as proof that I was his mother,
while tears of gratitude to the sweet friend and to God flowed
down my cheeks and dropped on baby's face as he wonderingly
looked up trying to pick off the tears with his little dimpled
fingers, and thankfully enjoyed the proof. The men turned aside
and tears flowed down more than one rugged face.

Once more on her way, Sally found herself on a train crowded
with soldiers, some discharged, others on furlough, "and the released
prisoners, with their pale, cadaverous unshaven faces and their long,
unkempt hair, one from Andersonville, more emaciated and ragged
than the others." She tried to ease her discomfort by reflecting on
how badly treated were the Confederate prisoners as well but it hurt
to sit silently for fear of her accent giving her away and listen as
"maledictions and curses were hurled against my people."

Taking the wrong train at her final transfer point put Sally and
her baby in Montreal later than expected but she religiously followed her instructions to remain on board "until I should be claimed,
like a general-delivery letter." Every passenger had left the coach as
she and her child waited, watching breathlessly for her claimant.
Finally, she saw three men approaching, one of whom looked vaguely
familiar. Instinctively, she looked the other way as the men neared.
Then she heard one say: "Don't you know your husband, little one?"

Sally looked up aghast. Not only was the man before her dressed
in an English civilian suit of rough brown cloth, when she was so
accustomed to George's Confederate gray uniform, but to her startled
disappointment his long curls that were so characteristic of him had
been shorn to alter his appearance dramatically.

As if in a dream, she found herself being swept away by carriage
along with her husband's companions — a Mr. Corse, a banker who
was a brother of Brig. Gen. Montgomery Corse, and a Mr. Symington,
who was a refugee from Baltimore — to a palatial home. There they
were greeted by a stately English butler and a pretty French maid
who took her baby from her aching arms. In minutes she surrendered herself to exhaustion, waking up an eternity later on a sofa
dressed in a pretty, soft, silken robe.

What they were doing in such a luxurious setting she could not
imagine. In a sense, it was a dream for the master of this mansion,
Mr. James Hutton, an old friend of Pickett's, had been summoned to
England and had made his home available to the Picketts just while
he was gone.

On the Huttons' return some weeks later, they had to give up their sumptuous digs, however, and with their modest means seek shelter elsewhere. They settled on a small boarding house maintained by an inquisitive French-Canadian woman with a varied clientele, from businessmen to traveling theatrical performers. The house had a wide veranda overlooking a court where the couple waited out the long days of their exile in quiet conversation and boredom. Meals were provided them in their single room except on Sundays when food was prepared in advance and set on a buffet in the dining room for all the guests to serve themselves. When she saw her humbled husband, plate in hand, helping himself at these weekly communal repasts, Sally said: "I could not help thinking of the time when once George had been served by butlers and waiters, each anxious to be the first to anticipate his wishes...I wondered how any one of those obsequious attendants would feel to see us now."[12]

They were living under the name Edwards and had told the mistress of the house little of their background. She appeared to grow more and more suspicious of who it was she had taken under her roof — particularly after the Picketts were paid a visit there by the governor general of Canada. Soon the expatriates became uneasy about their safety. They had heard of cases of Southern sympathizers being forcibly taken back across the border by Federal agents. They decided they had better change locations once more and packed their few belongings.

Ultimately, the investigation of the Kinston executions that Secretary of War Stanton had initiated became the responsibility of three junior (and doubtlessly very surprised and self-conscious) officers who happened to be serving in New Bern at the time. The three—Capt. W. H. Doherty, an assistant quartermaster; Capt. Burton S. Mills of the 14th United States Colored Artillery, Heavy; and 2nd Lt. Jonathan Hopkins, another white officer of the same regiment—were named by Brevet Major General Thomas H. Ruger on Oct. 19, 1865—six months after Appomattox—as a board of inquiry to convene as soon as practicable "to inquire into and report upon the circumstances connected with the alleged murder of a large number of U. S. soldiers by the rebels" early in the previous year.[13]

There had been a good deal of publicity in both the Northern and the Southern press about the episode and the officers were no doubt aware of the furor it had caused and the attention that would be focused on their deliberations and findings. It could hardly be looked

upon as welcome duty, any more than would be any other court assignment. It was something to be handled in a businesslike, dutiful manner and disposed of as promptly as possible.

Obviously, there had been a good deal of preliminary investigative work performed in and around Kinston before the board was even formed because only twelve days after its appointment the panel was ready to hear witnesses.

Initially, Captain Doherty, serving as president, convened the panel in New Bern. He summoned for testimony several widows of men who had been executed. It was a considerable distance for them to go and a journey for which the rustic, destitute farm women most probably had to be provided military escorts. Several Kinston residents were also subpoenaed to appear for the examination.

First to be sworn was Mrs. Catherine Summerlin, who had been left with five children to raise on her own when her husband Jesse was put to death. The simple woman, unaccustomed to having such attention focused on her, was no doubt ill at ease in the hushed hearing room as the Yankee officers began to question her, drawing her back to an event that remained to her — and so many others swept up in it — unreal, yet with every detail indelibly impressed in her memory. She could recall standing by the platform and not having the strength to watch further as she sensed the moment of execution — after all the dreary music and ritualistic preparation — had come. She knew her man was gone when "I heard the scaffold fall from under him," she told the court.

Many of the twelve men put to death with her husband were pine-woods neighbors, part of a culture and life-style strange and detached from that of the Kinston dwellers, men whose families were being left to mourn their loss in the isolation they preferred and always had sought to maintain. One of them, William Haddock, as a final bequest, "gave me his clothes to give to his mother," Mrs. Summerlin related, offering the officers a glimpse of the condition of these families, a state in which serviceable clothing was not put to waste in a grave.

Her obvious bitterness toward the Confederate authorities did not stem from the loss of her husband alone. While he was being held in jail, a party of soldiers under a Colonel Baker had ridden out to her place, some 20 miles from town, and confiscated her horse and her provisions for the winter. What was she left with to feed her family, someone asked her. "They took all I had," the widow stated plainly.

The court was particularly interested in Jesse Summerlin's status and whether he had freely enlisted in the Confederate army at any time prior to his joining the Union forces. He was conscripted, she insisted: "...there was an armed party come to his house and took him away by force."[14]

Mrs. Elizabeth Jones, the second witness, told of how her husband, Stephen, was mistreated at the jail, being forced to sleep on the bare floor. When asked if she had made any attempt to intercede with the rebel authorities on his behalf, she responded: "No, I did not; I was told it would be useless."[15]

Through her testimony and that of others to follow, it soon became obvious to the court that the military had taken over the town. Though its actions involved residents of that locale and were being carried out within its borders—even to the point of utilizing public buildings—it was clear to all that no civilian meddling was tolerated.

It seemed important for the board to know the military standing of the executed men at the time they were arrested and Mrs. Jones was pressed on that point as well. Her husband had at first volunteered for Confederate service, she admitted. And how long was he in that service? "He was in a number of times, but was sickly and discharged; the last time he was taken by force — conscripted." When asked if her husband deserted from the Rebel service, she replied, "He did, and he came inside the Union lines and enlisted in the Union army." Finally, the widow — as angry as the first one heard — was asked the names of Confederate officers in Kinston at the time and she was able to say, "I saw General Hoke; I think he was in command at the time."[16]

Two other widows were heard: Mrs. Nancy Jones, another mother of five, told of her difficulty in obtaining a conveyance to bring home the body of her husband, William, and Mrs. Celia Jane Brock recounted the story of how her husband, John, and the other men had been without food during their incarceration.

As the thrust of the questioning began to take shape, A. N. Daniels, a harness maker, was pressed for detailed information on the number of men executed and the dates, his understanding of who was in command, who were the executioners and how were the prisoners treated. It was his impression that the men had fared well in captivity, at least after their plight became known, "for the neighbors provided for them."[17]

On Wednesday, Nov. 1, the court reconvened and proceeded to examine the county jailer, Isaiah Wood, who believed he had been present at all the executions. He said of the disposal of the bodies

that "some of them were carried off by their friends; the others were buried at the foot of the gallows." He didn't help the board in fixing the exact number of men put to death because in addition to those hanged, he testified, "there were some that were shot, but I do not know how many."[18]

After hearing several other townsmen, who provided little specific information aside from the names of men they recognized who had been executed, Captain Doherty called a halt for the day. J. H. Dibble, the Northern-born carriage maker who had been imprisoned for his Union leanings, began the next day's testimony by placing both Hoke and Pickett at Kinston. O. S. Dewey, who had been the post quartermaster for the Confederate forces, was brought over from High Point to confirm that those two officers were the ones who were in command of the situation. But Dewey, too, confused the tally of men executed by saying that all he had personally observed "was the execution of two colored men, shot by order of Colonel Williams."[19]

This testimony only added to the confusion, for no reports existed of black men being put to death, as well. It is also unclear whether he was talking about Union soldiers or civilians. But the court moved on, and tried to preserve an element of focus on what seemed to be a state of mayhem.

The following Tuesday, the court moved to Kinston. As they rode down now deserted Queen Street, the Union officers could not have sensed what the town was like during the war. Gone were the loitering gray-clad soldiers crowding the piazzas, the noisy bar rooms, the bustle of war-time commerce. The ruined state of the economy was evident in the number of abandoned businesses and shattered spirits of the townspeople revealed in the blank, sullen expressions they showed their conquerors. The war had come to Kinston again in the last month of conflict when troops under General Hoke encountered elements of General J. M. Schofield's army at Southwest Creek while trying to reach Goldsboro and hook up with Gen. Joe Johnston's bedraggled Army of Tennessee. When Hoke withdrew, the town was once more occupied by Union troops, who became the paying patrons of its saloons and brothels.

Down by the river, the ill-fated ram, the *Neuse*, had been burned to avoid capture after never having done battle and its blackened timbers remained visible. But the real scars of Kinston's experience in the war were not as apparent, the psychological wounds of having been forced to host one of the most brutal episodes of the struggle.

The gallows had long been dismantled but could be clearly conjured by each of the residents whenever they happened near that open field in back of the jail.

Just where the board convened is uncertain but the Lenoir County Court House would be the likeliest meeting place and it may well have been that the officers sat at the very table where the seven-member Confederate court martial had gathered the previous year to deal so expeditiously with the deserters paraded before it.

The first witness called was clearly one of the most important the board would interview. He may have given the young officers a start as he approached the witness chair. They observed that he had suffered a disfiguring wound about his face that had cost him the sight of one eye. The witness was Lt. Col. Nethercutt, the former sheriff of Jones County who, after the execution of the men who had left his ranks, had gone to Virginia with the 66th North Carolina Regiment they had shunned. Only weeks after his arrival, he had been struck by a shell fragment at Petersburg.

Nethercutt was asked first what the men had been told when they had enlisted in his company of what he called "partisan rangers." "General Ransom stated to them that probably they would never be removed," the scarred veteran recalled. "This was when the company was first mustered in the service." Asked to clarify whether the general meant the state or that locality, Nethercutt responded, "As I understood it, not out of the locality."

When the unit was incorporated in the 66th North Carolina some time later, he explained that, "there was a great deal of dissatisfaction." As to what he thought caused the men to desert, he said that, "I think all they wanted was an excuse; don't think their sympathies were with the rebellion," was Nethercutt's reply by Lieutenant Hopkins' notes, though it would seem odd that Nethercutt would have used that hated word "rebellion" rather than secession. In closing, Nethercutt recounted his appeal to Hoke to have his men reprieved and how he was told by Hoke that he had an order for the execution that had to be carried out.

Under orders. But this officer was a brigadier general. To what extremes can an order go — and to what level of authority — before someone is held responsible for not objecting and disobeying the command? The officers on the board may well have pondered this question, as many in the military have before and since.

Nethercutt was then asked who gave the order for execution, and he offered in conclusion: "I can't swear; I think General Hoke told me it came from General Pickett, in command of Eastern North

Carolina."[20] The colonel stepped down and strode uncertainly from the room and returned to his home (where less than two years later he would be murdered in front of his family by two negroes at the instigation of the Carpetbag sheriff who had succeeded him).[21]

William S. Pope, now the provisional sheriff of Lenoir County, was more definite in fixing responsibility. When asked if he had heard the order for the executions read, he responded: "I did; it was by order of General Pickett."[22]

The next day, the court heard for the first time of the mysterious hangman from Raleigh. Merchant Aaron Baer described the volunteer executioner as "a man about six feet high, stout, cross-eyed." But the board, probe as it did, never was able to establish his identity and could only wonder in what base corner of society such a disgusting character would disappear.[23]

Baer was followed by the foundry owner and carriage maker, James B. Webb, who gave the tribunal its first information that the men actually had received a trial of any sort. "I was present at a meeting which I was told was a court martial and trying William Haddock," he related. His testimony was confirmed by the blacksmith, Bryan McCullum, although it was by way of conveying his anger at not having the lawyer he had procured for his brother-in-law's trial being admitted.[24]

The board returned to New Bern to sift through the often vague and inconsistent testimony that Lt. Hopkins had transcribed from the procession of 28 witnesses who had appeared, many eagerly seeking retribution, others reluctant to indicate to the Federal officers the extent of their involvement in Confederate affairs.

From the exercise, the panel had been able to establish the basic facts about the episode, much of which, unbeknownst to the court, Pickett had freely admitted in his correspondence with General Peck. It could then color in the circumstances in which the executions were carried out. The findings might have been more helpful as a basis for further action had the tone of the court's report been somewhat less strident and some of the adjectives, employed for emphasis, sacrificed.

While documenting the rough treatment of the prisoners and their families, what the three officers had not addressed was the legal culpability of the Confederate leaders involved, leaving to others the task of making a case. Still, they left little doubt of their sentiments as they phrased their conclusions:

> After the capture of these men at Beech Grove, (sic) North Carolina, they were confined in the court house at Kinston, N. C., until they were removed to the dungeon of the old jail at the

same town where they remained until they were executed under most cruel and debasing treatment, and were rescued from starvation only by their friends supplying them with food.

Nor did the outrages perpetrated upon the victims of the wholesale slaughter cease with cruel treatment or with death itself.

These dead bodies were stripped of their clothing almost or quite to a state of nudity, to be contemptuously left for relatives to gather up and inter, delivered to experimenting surgery, like a common felon, or scooped into a common grave at the foot of the gallows, while their families were insulted, robbed of their property, and left to depend upon the charity of friends (while they who befriended them were themselves in danger).

The board was satisfied that the men had been tried by court martial but "has been unable to learn who comprised this court, or by whose order it was convened, though it was thought to have been comprised of officers belonging to Virginia organizations. The testimony of J. H. Nethercutt proves, conclusively, that these men belonged to the local North Carolina service, and that they never had been Confederate soldiers," the board observed. "Therefore, in the opinion of the board, a Confederate States court martial had no jurisdiction over them."

It also ventured the opinion "that further investigation would prove that Elijah Kellum never had been either in the local or Confederate service, but that he was fraudulently reported as conscripted by a Captain Wilson, of Jones County, N. C., enrolling officer in the rebel service."

The panel went on to cite the testimony of various witnesses to establish that:

> *the rebel General Pickett was in command of the department of eastern North Carolina and approved the sentence of death passed by the above mentioned court and ordered the execution of these United States soldiers and General Hoke, in command of Kinston, N. C., was charged with the execution, by the agency of Pickett's provost guard and several voluntary hangmen, one of whom is known as Blunt King of Goldsboro, N. C. The person who hung the 13 is known as a tall, dark-complexioned man, with a cross or squint eye, a resident of Raleigh, N. C. His name the board has been unable to learn.*
>
> *The proof of the unparalleled barbarities of the last two men, above mentioned, is very positive and abundant.*

In approaching its recommendations, the board stated that:

> ...*the object of this disgraceful sacrifice of human life, in the opinion of the board, perpetrated on the part of the leaders was to terrify the loyal people of North Carolina, to make them subservient to their foul scheme of rebellion, and to bring contempt upon the government its victims represented, of which the slaughter of the friends and neighbors of these loyal people, the contempt shown to the persons and property of the widows...is sufficient evidence.*

Those directly implicated were, in the board's view, the members of the court martial, Pickett, Hoke, a Colonel Baker and the two hangmen. In closing, the panel stated:

> *It is the opinion of the board that these men have violated the rules of war and every principle of humanity, and are guilty of crimes too heinous to be excused by the United States government and, therefore, that there should be a military commission immediately appointed for the trial of these men, and to inflict upon the perpetrators of such crimes their just punishment.*[25]

Just as the work of establishing the facts in the case had trickled down from high authority in Washington to three junior officers, their determination began a slow ascent through channels, the report being read first by the appointing officer, General Thomas H. Ruger. It was then forwarded to the capital where it reached the hands of the judge advocate general, Joseph Holt, a former Democrat from Kentucky now much in league with the Republican radicals. Holt currently was beginning to draw criticism for his extensive use of military commissions to supplant the normal judicial processes, such as that which had just tried the Lincoln conspirators.

Mr. Holt, as head of the Bureau of Military Justice, went over the board of inquiry findings carefully and then presented his views to the secretary of war on what further steps should be taken. He observed to Mr. Stanton that:

> ...*the record furnished no evidence that the unhappy victims of this outrage were not deserters, so far as an abandonment of a constrained and hated service would warrant their being stigmatized as such, but on the contrary, the little evidence on that point furnished by the record tends to show that they were....*
>
> *In respect, however, to the monstrous barbarity and guilt involved in the execution of these Union soldiers, it is of little*

(Library of Congress)

Judge Advocate General Joseph Holt.

consequence whether or not they had, before entering into the service of the United States, fled from the despotic servitude of a rebel conscription.... Submission to that service was, in itself, a crime from which it was their bounden duty, as men and as patriots, to flee at the first opportunity.

Though he may well have been placing the issue on a far higher plane of duty and righteousness than old Joe Haskett, Holt argued that John Brock and the others who were executed may have had idealistic motivations when they went into the Union camp. Holt rounded out his argument to Stanton by asserting:

Having so fled and taken service and shelter under their country's flag they were entitled to the protection of that country so long as it could be extended to them, and to its ample vengeance upon their oppressors and murderers for their shameful death, inflicted, as it was, under circumstances of contumely and ferocious cruelty rarely equalled by savages.

But, having expressed all this outrage, Mr. Holt came to a surprisingly restrained and decidedly judicial conclusion:

While it is the opinion of this office that every sentiment of patriotism and public justice forbids that the blood of these murdered men should cry in vain from their dishonored graves for vengeance, it finds in the evidence submitted to it no grounds upon which personal charges could be established and sustained against the guilty parties.

He explained that "there was no evidence before the court of inquiry showing conclusively by whom or by whose order these sufferers were arrested and prosecuted; by whom tried, condemned, or executed." The judge advocate concluded:

It is recommended, therefore, by this office, that the papers in the case be returned to the commanding general of the department of North Carolina, with instructions to cause further and minute investigations to be made into the circumstances of the case, with the view of tracing and fixing the guilt of its lawless and savage transactions upon individuals who can be held responsible for them; collecting testimony that will likely establish such guilt. And, in case the investigation should prove successful, to prepare charges against such parties, and forthwith appoint a military commission for their trial.[26]

It was obvious that up to this point neither the board of inquiry nor Judge Advocate General Holt was aware of the exchange of correspondence between General Pickett and General Peck. Consequently, a good deal of time was wasted establishing facts that had been, in effect, stipulated. However, when Peck, writing from his home in Syracuse, N. Y., made the extent of his knowledge known, the entire complexion of the investigation changed and Holt's attitude altered abruptly. On Dec. 30, 1865, seventeen days after his previous appraisal of the situation was sent to Stanton, he amended his assessment dramatically, explaining:

There was no evidence in the papers then under consideration showing conclusively by whom, or by whose order, these sufferers were arrested, condemned, or slain; but a letter of inquiry addressed by this office to General Peck, then commanding North Carolina, led him to refer to a correspondence held by him with General Pickett, of the rebel army in February 1864. It will be seen from copies of this correspondence, which is submitted herewith, that the letters of General Pickett of 16th

and 17th February supply, to a large extent, the deficiency of evidence referred to.

Not only does the imperious and vaunting temper in which these letters are written indicate his readiness to commit this or any kindred atrocity, but his boastful admission that he was in command at the time, that the 22 men, of whose names he furnishes a list, had been executed, and his threat that he would retaliate in the proportion of ten to one by executions among the 450 officers and men whom he says "I have in my hands, and subject to my order," all tend to show that he was in responsible command and furnish evidence upon which it is believed charges can be sustained against him.

It is therefore recommended that these additional papers be transmitted to the general commanding, to be used in connection with such other evidence as may result from the investigation now in progress; and when the preparation of the case shall have been completed, charges be preferred against the said G. E. Pickett, and such other persons as may be shown to have been in complicity with him in these murders, and their trial ordered. As a preliminary step to such trial it is suggested that Pickett be at once arrested and held to await it, upon the evidence furnished in his correspondence adverted to, which is deemed abundantly sufficient to warrant such arrest.[27]

But while filling one gap in his understanding of the situation, Holt remained unaware that George Pickett had long ago fled the country and was living under an assumed name in Canada, thanks to the timely alert of his high-ranking chums in the army of the government that was now moving more vigorously against him.

Demonstrating his mounting venom, Holt got off another letter to Mr. Stanton the same day in which he enclosed a copy of one of Pickett's self-incriminating letters to Peck. Holt opined: "Were this paper referred to the Attorney General, it is thought that its temper and avowals might assist in determining the question of the writer's pardon, which is said to be pending before the President. I shall recommend the arrest and trial of Pickett for the murder of the 22 Union prisoners of war who were executed under his authority."[28]

Lest they need any further prodding, the earnest young captain who had headed the first inquiry, Captain Doherty, took the liberty of following up his report by writing to both Judge Advocate Holt and then Secretary of War Stanton himself to urge that they actively pursue Pickett. To Holt, Doherty sought to make the point that:

...it would strengthen the hands of the Government immensely, could this bad and cruel man be brought to condign punishment, and our poor, murdered soldiers be avenged.... I thus venture to trouble you, because I know you share my feelings of indignation at this horrid crime, and I know that a lasting disgrace will attach to the United States Government if it is permitted to pass unpunished. The poor whites of the South will lose confidence in the federal power if thus forsaken and their murdered friends unavenged.

To Stanton, the determined junior officer asserted: "The authors of this inhuman murder shall be brought to trial.... Thus only can the honor of the Government be vindicated, and the cruel enemies of the Union punished, and the friends of the federal authority sustained and encouraged in these Southern States."[29]

The new board of inquiry that Holt had called for to take another look into the executions of the 2nd North Carolina men and "to fix the guilt of their murders on individuals who can be held responsible" was made up of three lieutenants — identified as Asa Bird Gardner, adjutant of the 7th Regiment Veteran Reserve Corps, George H. Penniman of the 28th Michigan Infantry and William R. Wilcox, also of the 28th Michigan. What the members may have lacked in maturity they made up in energy and determination.

After being convened on Jan. 17, 1866 in Raleigh, now the headquarters of the army's Department of North Carolina, the three shavetails immediately began pawing through the previous testimony and findings and undertook trips to Salisbury, Goldsboro, Kinston, New Bern, Halifax, Beaufort and other localities in quest of witnesses and documents to pin the responsibility for the hangings on particular individuals. They made personal inquiries of members of the state legislature, the secretary of state, the governor and whoever they thought might be likely to afford information. The records of the state adjutant general's office, contained in many large boxes, were examined painstakingly to determine if the names of the hanged men appeared on muster rolls of certain units and what the nature of those units was.

The board saw little point in recalling witnesses previously examined by the first board and sought to go beyond accumulating further grisly details on the executions. But information was not easy to come by. "Great distaste was quite generally exhibited by the witnesses to testify, lest they might be considered by their friends

in the light of 'informers,'" the board's report noted. "Defective memories seemed to be prevalent in reference to occurrences at the particular times specified—the witnesses alleging, however, with some show of reason, that the exciting military events then constantly succeeding each other unremittedly did not permit these particular ones to make deep impressions."[30] The problem the board was to have in evidence gathering became immediately apparent when it met on Jan. 29 to begin hearing testimony and had to adjourn "in consequence of the non-attendance of witnesses."[31]

The next day, through some manner of persuasion, the board had before it a 30-year-old printer, John B. Neathery of Raleigh, who as a lieutenant had served during much of the war as an assistant to the adjutant general of North Carolina. As such, it soon became clear, he knew a great deal of how the Confederate forces were organized. Neathery recalled that he "was in Kinston a few days after the execution in April and recollect the people expressed great regret at the execution, feeling that it was for a small offense" though which one he was alluding to was not established.

Of the nature of service of Nethercutt's battalion, the witness said that "as 'partisan rangers' they could not be removed out of their immediate section. When they were found to be of little use, an order was issued for their transfer to the 66th regiment. The order was considered as violation of the terms of their enlistment, and objected to by the men."

The protest, he explained, was dealt with in pragmatic fashion. "They were given their choice of going into the 66th regiment," he said, "or being mustered out and conscripted, which amounted to the same thing—'whipping the devil around the stump.'" In the view of the Confederate authorities, Neathery said, "it was considered merely a change of position on paper, as they would have been sent to the regiment all the same under the Confederate conscript laws."

As it turned out, many of the men transferred to the 66th without their consent were discharged by habeas corpus orders from the supreme court of the state. This occurred after someone more knowledgeable about the law than the draftees ever would be had advised them to apply for such writs.

"Partisan rangers," in general, were abolished late in 1863, Neathery remembered, mainly because "it was considered one of the most perfect ways to avoid conscription." Those men who did not succeed in obtaining writs and had been "dragooned into the service," Neathery said, "succeeded in effecting their escape to the woods.

My impression is that they were not allowed to return to their homes; the pressure was for men, and they were compelled to consent to go into the 66th or to be discharged and conscripted on the spot into the regiment; the whole thing was on paper, and ultimately meant service in the 66th any way."[32]

From Neathery's testimony, and that of Colonel Nethercutt contained in the record of the previous court, the board had a pretty clear idea of what sort of soldiers the men of the 2nd North Carolina, U. S. A., were. But it would be up to others to decide whether such indifferent recruits deserved what became of them because of the course they had taken to minimize their involvement in the war.

George Snow, a 19-year-old saw mill operator residing in Raleigh, had been a lieutenant and aide-de-camp to Brig. Gen. Martin during the war and was able to relate the experience of Nethercutt's battalion after it was incorporated in the 66th North Carolina. When asked how many members of the unit had gone into the regiment, he estimated "not half of them," and when questioned whether it was not generally understood at headquarters that it required a considerable force to keep this regiment together, the young man had to respond: "Yes, sir; Nethercutt had some men he could trust, who did guard duty, and who would have died for him."

Once brought up to Virginia, the regiment did well, he thought. "They fought like men at Coal (Cold) Harbor," he related. "A good many of the 66th afterwards joined the regiment, seeing the error of their ways; they would come in by squads, as the regiment was a long while in the state."[33]

When Samuel McDonald Tate, the former lieutenant colonel of the 6th North Carolina, was called, he was routinely asked his current occupation and he responded rather smugly: "My occupation is that of a gentleman." Later he would become the president of a small railroad in his state but this phrasing was probably his genteel way of saying he was at present without employment.

Tate's testimony was often difficult to follow because it appeared so much at variance with what either board of inquiry had heard about the executions. For example, when asked if he could recollect the execution of any deserters in Kinston, he responded: "Yes, sir; about seventy-odd." Though there was ample evidence that many more than the 22 deaths being investigated had occurred, no one else had indicated that the grand total would approach what the colonel was estimating.

When asked how many executions he had attended, Tate said: "Three or more. They began and increased until they got to be fright-

ful." The court waited while he labored over his arithmetic. "I think there were twenty-odd hung at the first time, but I am not positive to more than twelve, as I wish to be particular. In our service we shot a man for desertion; but for desertions to the enemy, which was a higher offense, we hung them, and that is why I think these men were hung." It was quite clear to him that "the court was ordered by General Pickett."[34]

Another curious witness was a lawyer from New Bern, John Hughes. He had been the quartermaster of Hoke's Brigade and, as such, had been left in Virginia in charge of baggage and transportation when the brigade embarked for his home town. He caught up with his unit in Kinston on the day that the thirteen men were executed and, his legal instincts stirred, started to ask questions about what had led to this. "I witnessed the execution, which was conducted in the usual form, in the presence of all the troops then in the vicinity of Kinston, the condemned being attended and ministered to at the time of their execution by the brigade chaplain," the attorney recalled. "The reason why I made the inquiry was, I was a lawyer and felt interested in the matter; it was the only execution by hanging I had ever witnessed in the army."

All he could determine to satisfy his curiosity that the slaughter he had viewed was legally performed was General Hoke's assurance that the men had been tried by a court martial. Hoke also affirmed that there was an "order from General G. E. Pickett ordering their execution."[35]

The most imposing witness to come before the board was probably Zebulon B. Vance, the popular war-time governor, who had little doubt that the men of Nethercutt's battalion had been abused. "I am inclined to think the Confederate government did not keep faith with these local troops, who were found to be of little, if any, benefit to the service," the handsome politician stated candidly. "I did at various times make appeals to Confederate authorities in behalf of men of this state. These men were enlisted entirely for local defense, and every effort was made to transfer these organizations into the regular service of the Confederacy when they were found to be worthless. I myself favored transfer to regular service where it could be done without violations of good faith, but though in these instances of Nethercutt's battalion it was a violation of their enlistment agreements."[36]

Twenty-one-year-old John G. Justice of Lincolnton, N. C., the home of General Hoke and another prominent Confederate leader, Gen. Stephen Dodson Ramseur, admitted under questioning that as

a lieutenant under Hoke he had stood on the scaffold and had to read the sentence of execution aloud to the assembled troops before one group of men was hanged. But when asked if he was also present when the thirteen were executed, the young man rather ashamedly said: "I staid in my quarters then."

Justice also recalled that his brigade kept a special order book in which court martial proceedings were copied and that he had "tried to look it up the day I received my summons to appear here but could not find it; the book was lost at the surrender."[37] The court may well have wondered whether there was any paper record anywhere of what had been done there.

Even old John Cobb Washington had been located by the dogged inquisitors to testify, though he was inclined to minimize his station in Kinston at the time and what influence he might have had over the proceedings had he chosen to interfere. He described himself simply as "a planter" who was "frequently at home in Kinston, though travelling considerably" in 1864.

When asked of any conversation he ever held with any of the officers of the Confederate army concerning the executions, the town's most affluent citizen and leader of the secession movement there replied: "I have no recollection of any. General Pickett was once or twice at my house; General Hoke frequently, and other officers."

When the hangings were actually taking place, Washington said he stood a hundred or two hundred yards distant of the gallows. The court then asked him to, "State whether there was any conversation among the people of Kinston as to the justness of the hanging of these men, and the general opinion."

Now that was simply too much to ask of a man in his position, Washington implied when he answered: "My impression is that there was considerable, but being removed from such intercourse with them, I cannot recall what it was."[38]

When George W. Quinn of Kinston, who had been a courier for Gen. Seth Barton, was asked his view of the sentiments of the townspeople about what was going on, his reply was "that these men ought not to have been hung." According to Quinn, "They belonged to Nethercutt's battalion and enlisted, so it was believed, on a distinct promise, as several of the men of that battalion told me, that they were never to be sent above the Wilmington and Weldon railroad and that their commander, Major Nethercutt, made this promise."[39]

Blunt King was brought over from Goldsboro where he was now assistant chief of police to provide his damning testimony about George Pickett's determination to deal harshly with the deserters to

set an example. But he probably shocked the court more with his callous description of his own involvement in the executions. It was surprising, indeed, that a man who did the work of a hangman so indifferently should be the one to establish the "animus," as the court would call it, of another.

After listening to several other witnesses provide clearly irrelevant testimony, the court—two months after beginning its far-reaching investigation—concluded that it was unlikely to develop anything further of significance. It framed its report to the department commander, while all too aware that its findings were destined for much higher authority. In this report, considerable attention was given to the status of Nethercutt's battalion as a "local defense" unit. "The evidence shows that this class of troops were found to be of little or no service, that men volunteered therein for the purpose of being out of danger, avoiding conscription and remaining near their homes—a feeling which caused little sympathy for them among the rank and file of the rebel army," the three lieutenants stated plainly. Consolidation of the battalion into a regular regiment "was distasteful to Nethercutt's men, and that considering it was violating the terms of their enlistment, many took to the woods and deserted, and coming into the Union lines, enlisted in the 2nd North Carolina loyal volunteers."

The question of the Confederate government's right to conscript these members of units such as Nethercutt's, the board looked upon as a legal issue beyond its purvue. "How far the so-called Confederate government had the belligerent right to discharge its enlisted men of these local defense battalions from service, and conscript them on the spot for general service on refusal to enter voluntarily into the 66th, this board did not feel called upon to determine," was the way the point was addressed.

When it came to fixing responsibility for the executions—the primary mission of the board—the members showed no such reluctance to state their views in direct, unequivocal terms:

> *The board are therefore of the opinion that the rebel Major General G. E. Pickett, commanding the department of eastern North Carolina in 1864, in the language of the Judge Advocate General, "was the guilty party by whom or by whose order these sufferers were arrested and prosecuted, and by whose order executed."*
>
> *The board regret their inability, after diligent search, to prove "by whom these men were tried and condemned."*
>
> *The evidence taken tends towards showing that the court*

martial before which they were brought was a general court martial ordered by General Pickett....

While other prominent rebels seem to have been concerned in these shameful transactions as accessories, the evidence clearly shows that General Pickett was the prominent authority under whose direction everything connected with the murder of our soldiers took place; and the board are therefore unable, from the evidence they have been able to collect, to fix the guilt upon any subordinate in such a manner as to contain grounds sufficient for preferring personal charges. [40]

That the findings of these junior officers were being anxiously awaited at a level far higher than their own is indicated by a resolution adopted on the floor of the U. S. House of Representatives only two weeks after the report was filed. It demanded:

...that the Secretary of War be directed to communicate to this house a report of the Judge Advocate General, and such other information as may be of record or on file in his department on the subject, which will show what are the facts in the case, and what steps have been taken to bring to justice and punishment the murderers of the following named Union soldiers...alleged to have been tried and executed by orders of the rebel generals Pickett and Hoke under the pretext of their being deserters from the Confederate service.... [41]

CHAPTER SIX
"But he made you immortal"

A change of digs may have made George and Sally Pickett feel a bit more secure but it also added to his sense of deprivation from the only life that he had known, a military one. The family's new rooms opened on the Champs de Mars in Montreal and from the windows George could look out and see troops, albeit in strange uniforms, drilling on the field below.

"We stood at the window and watched the soldiers, keeping time with them to step and tune outwardly, while hiding the muffled sound within, each playing we were enjoying it, without one marring thought of the crumpled-browed past, trying to fool each other till we really fooled ourselves," Sally would recall of those days. "It was with thankfulness that I saw the General watch with unfeigned interest the maneuvers of the soldiers, day after day, and pleasantly welcome reveille and tattoo. Our baby learned to march almost before he walked."

"In spite of poverty, fears for the future and grief for the past," Sally thought they had managed to maintain their spirits well in their extended exile, until George became very ill. At the same time, their son came down with croup but friends relieved her of the baby while she devoted herself to her husband. The medical bills multiplied without her paying much attention until when "our board bill was sent up, I counted over our little store and found there was not enough left to meet it."

Secreting the invoice from her husband, the young wife put on her bonnet, went down to the office and asked for her deposit box from the safe. After removing a set of emeralds, she asked the proprietor "to direct me to the most reliable jeweler and to send someone to sit with my husband until my return."

Sally admitted to "very little experience in buying of merchants, and none whatever in selling to them." She remembered her uneasiness when a clerk led her to a gray-haired man with something that "very much resembled a napkin-ring screwed into his right eye" as he studied some jewels lying on a tray before him, a man who "wore his teeth on the outside of his mouth."

The jeweler's initial response to his attractive client was to announce that "we don't hemploy young women 'ere" but when she explained her purpose, his tact changed to "this is not a pawnbroker's shop either, mum." When Sally displayed her earrings, however, his question became, "Where did you get these hemerlds from, miss?" With what was left of her pride, Sally replied, "I was born with them, sir."

Much to her further embarrassment, the proprietor would not believe the young woman and sent his clerk with her back to her hotel to verify her residence and ownership of the gems. The manager of the hotel was equally indignant that one of his guests was being so insulted and insisted, after disposing of the jeweler's young assistant, that Sally not bother herself with the bill for her room. "Mr. Edwards and I will arrange all that when he is well—entirely well," the hosteler asserted.

While George's health gradually improved, their financial situation did not. Sally seemed to be more concerned about it than he for it was she who was actively addressing their plight. One day she happened to notice an advertisement in the newspaper for a teacher of Latin in Miss McIntosh's school and the spunky young mother decided to answer it.

Arriving at the private school, Sally was confronted by a tall and angular woman with "grizzly-red hair arranged in three large puffs (like fortifications I thought) on each side of her long, thin face, high cheek-bones, Roman nose and eyes crowded up together under gold-rimmed spectacles." When she referred to the ad, Sally was told that it was "for a teacher, not for a pupil."

Despite the woman's skepticism, the applicant did finally get to meet the professor who was going abroad and was in need of a replacement to instruct 14 girls, all of whom appeared older than she. He asked first where Sally had been educated and she answered "at home, except two years, sir. Then I went to Lynchburg College, where I was graduated."

"Is that in England?"

"Oh, no sir."

The teacher said his class had just finished Caesar and asked Sally how it commences. When she quickly responded, "Gallia est omnis divisa in partes tres," he was encouraged to give her a few sentences to translate, than an ode from Horace and some selections from Catullus and Tibullus before announcing, "I will engage you, Mrs. Edwards, and will be responsible for you."

Her idle husband did not know where she went every day, while he stayed at home. Nor was he aware that her first month's salary

was spent in part payment for an overcoat for him as the severe Canadian winter began to envelop them.[1]

While he was living out of the country under his assumed name, entreaties continued to be made in Washington on Pickett's behalf. On November 3, Orville Browning received a letter in Washington from Pickett's sister, Mrs. Burwell of Richmond, inquiring if nothing could be done to secure George's long-delayed pardon so that he might feel safe to return and enter into business. In response, Browning noted in his diary that he:

> ...*went this morning to Genl Grant's Head Qtrs to consult with him. We both thought it inexpedient to apply for a pardon just now, but Genl Grant said he could go where he pleased, and engage in any business he pleased, and he should not be molested—that those who surrendered with Genl Lee, and were paroled were not subject to Indictment, and he felt it his duty to protect them from molestation on account of any act prior to that time, and that he had directed an order to be issued and published relieving them all from their paroles so far as to enable them to go when and where they pleased, and to embark in any business that was open to them — that it was the interest of the government to get them all engaged in industrial pursuits as soon as possible....*

What particularly impressed Browning, apparently, was Grant's concern with living up to the terms he had given General Lee, conditions that insisted that the surrendered officers and men "not be disturbed by U. S. authority so long as they observe their paroles and the laws in force where they may reside."

No exceptions had been stipulated. In their latest discussion of Pickett's situation, the commanding general stressed that:

> *He drew up the terms of surrender without consulting Genl Lee, and they were accepted just as drawn, and that good faith required that he should protect those who surrendered from prosecution and punishment, and he intended to do it—that we had got the benefit of the contract and must abide by it—that if terms had not been offered, Lee's army would have dispersed through the country in guerrilla bands and the war would not yet have been over & Genl Ingalls was present at this conversation.*[2]

It was all well and good for Sam Grant to define for Browning the spirit of his terms to Lee. But Pickett no doubt felt that some-

thing more personalized and specific to his situation was required before he could feel secure enough to return across the border. It did not come until four months after Browning's last visit to the commanding general and took the form of a pass signed by Grant himself and forwarded in a letter from George's close friend, Ingalls, on March 12, 1866.

The priceless pass stated plainly:

> *George E. Pickett, a paroled officer of the Southern Army, is exempt from arrest by military authorities, except directed by the President of the United States, Secretary of War or from their aides as long as he observes the conditions of his parole.*
>
> *The restriction requiring paroled officers to remain at their homes is removed in this case and General Pickett will be allowed to travel unmolested throughout the United States.[3]*

Considering the fact that the second board of inquiry into the Kinston executions had not yet completed its findings, having the commander of the army step into the matter at this time and guarantee the subject of the investigation safe conduct was a remarkable bit of interference. Grant was not taking his friend George completely off the hook but he was—by placing his signature on a piece of paper—making it possible for him to return home without worry of seizure except on highest authority.

With Grant's action, it was clear that the Pickett case had created a serious schism in the government. On the one hand, the secretary of war and the judge advocate general were using a military commission to bring to justice a Southern officer allegedly involved in what was being widely perceived as a gross atrocity. On the other hand, the commanding general was standing ready to disregard any such conduct for the sake of living up to the blanket terms he had offered to secure the surrender of the Army of Northern Virginia.

The largesse extended to the returning exiles was not limited to the assurance of safe conduct. Sally recalled of their long journey, one far less harrowing than her northern flight the year before:

> *We stopped in New York en route to Virginia, expecting to remain there only three or four days, but we found that our board had been paid in advance for two weeks, that a carriage had been put at our service for that length of time, and that in our box was a pack of wine-cards marked "Paid." To this day I*

General Ulysses S. Grant.

*do not know how many people's guests we were, for a great
many of General Pickett's old army friends were there at the
time, and they all vied with each other in making it pleasant
and happy for us.[4]*

Once back in Virginia, George first took his family to Turkey
Island. Although the main house was burned beyond repair, there
was a cottage nearby which they could occupy while he made an
effort at working the land. But at this endeavor, he soon showed
himself singularly inept. To make matters worse, a number of fellow Confederate officers, as destitute as he, straggled in to join him
at the agricultural effort and showed themselves no more suited, or

genuinely interested, in this mode of life. As Sally recalled of her husband's pathetic attempt at adjustment to the civilian world, "he tried to turn his sword into a plowshare, but he was not expert with plowshares." Of his unwelcome hands, she would say with disdain:

> *...they would rise at any hour that pleased them, linger over breakfast, and then go out to the fields. If the sun were too hot or the wind too cold, they would come back to sit on the veranda or around the fire till dinner was ready.*
>
> *There were generals, colonels, majors, captains, lieutenants, privates—all of one rank now; and he who desired a graphic history of the four years' war needed only to listen to the conversation of the agricultural army at Turkey Island. But the inevitable came; resources were in time exhausted, and proprietor and assistants were forced to seek other fields.*[5]

While trying to provide for his family, George had the distraction of the case still pending against him. With or without prior discussion with Grant, he decided to formulate a personal appeal that might serve as the basis for final disposition of the complaints and had it delivered to the commanding general. The document was an extraordinary piece of prose if only for the total reversal of tone that the decidedly reduced Pickett adopted from the arrogant manner he had displayed at the time of the executions and in his dealings with his counterpart, General Peck. Now it was a humble Pickett, presenting himself as just another soldier performing his duty, one with minimal involvement in the whole affair. Anyone who had been on the New Bern expedition and had observed his behavior toward his prisoners could have only retched at the way he now attempted—in his diminished state—to distance himself from the episode as he appealed to his friend to save his neck.

Pickett wrote the following entreaty:

> *I have the honor to state that shortly after the surrender of the Confederate forces under command of Gen. R. E. Lee to Gen. U. S. Grant, commander-in-chief, United States Army, in the past year, being at the time paroled by the last-named officer, I made a communication to his excellency the President of the United States.*
>
> *The papers in the case were presented by ex-Senator O. H. Browning, of Illinois, for the consideration of the Executive.*
>
> *They consisted of the application above referred to, the required oath, a recommendation from Gov. Pierpoint, of Virginia, and certain statements from officers of the Confederate service—*

members of a general court-marshal (sic)—in reference to the execution of a number of deserters from said service while I was in command of the Department of North Carolina in 1863.

My object now, General, in presenting this paper, is to ask your favorable consideration of my case, and that you will, if you believe in my sincerity, for which I have pledged you my honor as an officer and a gentleman, put such an indorsement upon it as will obtain from his Excellency the President a guarantee that I may be permitted to live unmolested in my native State, where I am now trying to make a subsistence for my family (much impoverished by the war), by tilling the land.

It has come to my knowledge that certain ill-disposed persons are attempting to re-open the troubles of the past, and embroil me for the action taken by me while the commanding officer of the Confederate forces in North Carolina.

I acted simply as the general commanding the Department.

Certain men, deserters from a North Carolina regiment, were taken with arms in their hands fighting against the colors under which they had enlisted.

Charges were proferred against them, a regularly organized court-marshal was assembled, composed of officers from North Carolina, Georgia and Virginia, before whom the men were tried. The evidence in the cases being perfectly unmistakeable, the men being identified by members of their old regimental comrades, they were found guilty and condemned to be hung.

The sentences were approved by me, and they were duly executed according to the custom of war in like cases. My action was sanctioned by the then Confederate Government. If the time has not arrived for the executive clemency to be extended to my case (and which point I am not now pressing), I merely wish some assurance that I will not be disturbed in my endeavors to keep my family from starvation, and that my parole, which was given in good faith, may protect me from the assaults of those persons desirous of still keeping up the war which has ended, in my humble opinion, forever.

Appealing to you as a soldier, and feeling confident you will appreciate my position, I sign myself, with much esteem, your obedient servant.[6]

Grant, whose so-called friends would cause him a good deal of embarrassment, did not even wait for the report of his own army's board of inquiry before chomping on his cigar and penning an endorsement to President Andrew Johnson:

Respectfully forwarded to his Excellency the President of the United States, with the recommendation that clemency be extended in this case, or assurances given that no trial will take place for the offenses charged against G. E. Pickett.

During the rebellion, belligerent rights were acknowledged to the enemies of our country, and it is clear to me that the parole given by the armies laying down their arms protects them against punishment for acts lawful for any other belligerent. In this case I know that it is claimed that the men tried and convicted for the crime of desertion were Union men from North Carolina, who had found refuge within our lines and in our service. The punishment was a harsh one, but it was in time of war, and when the enemy, no doubt, felt it necessary to retain by some power the services of every man within their reach.

General Pickett I know personally to be an honorable man, but in this case his judgment prompted him to do what cannot well be sustained, though I do not see how good, either to the friends of the deceased, or by fixing an example for the future, can be secured by his trial now. It would only open up the question whether or not the government did not disregard its contract entered into to secure the surrender of an armed enemy.[7]

The Pickett letter to which Grant was responding was hardly the first plea he had received concerning his case. Grant told a Congressional committee he had, "received one appeal after another, not only from Pickett himself and from his relations, but from officers of the Army, who knew him very well and favorably prior to the war."[8]

For all intents and purposes, Grant's intercession closed the matter. Pickett was not to be brought to trial, despite the recommendations of the board of inquiry and the judge advocate general and the clamoring in the House of Representatives. Grant was too powerful a man to mess with and his judgment was accepted by the president. What is more, there was not even a suggestion of reparations from any source for the destitute families of the executed men in his endorsement.

The commanding general's reasoning showed still one more instance of the manner in which the concept of honor was being distorted by the principals in the Kinston affair. Grant looked upon strict adherence to the terms he had signed in Wilmer McLean's parlor at Appomattox as a transcending point of honor, regardless of what information may come out subsequently about the conduct of the Southern officers covered by them. But surely he was aware of Pickett's presence at the surrender site at the time if the privates in

his ranks were. Similarly, he was aware of the accusations against the Virginian. The Kinston executions had received enough attention in the press. With Lee in no position to do anything but accept whatever terms were offered him, Grant should have stipulated that certain officers were to remain liable for prosecution if there was evidence connecting them with war crimes.

The explanation lies in the realm of regular army cronyism. The condemned rustics from North Carolina were ersatz soldiers who had presented a tough disciplinary problem, in Grant's view. Yes, it was too bad that Pickett had gone so far, but he was known for always making a show of things, with a taste for the dramatic. But he was of the academy, had fought like a madman in Mexico, and was "old army" to the core. Grant saw no sense in making too much of this thing; he saw Pickett as an honorable man, just an officer making a tough decision, doing his duty, and felt he should let it pass.

If Grant was unilaterally ready to close the book on the Kinston case, he had to pay the price of supporting his friend. There were those in the government who were furious that Pickett was not being brought to trial but none as incensed as Rush Hawkins, the wealthy New York attorney who as a Union colonel had recruited the North Carolinians and was himself, "though unwittingly, responsible for placing these murdered victims in a position which caused them to be assassinated." To Hawkins, "a more perfect and complete case of atrocious guilt was never proved in any court of law than is made out against this great criminal" in the transcripts of the boards of inquiry:

> *Testimony is multiplied to such an extent that the most common understanding cannot fail to identify the monster who ordered this Dahomean feast of murder, fit only to disgrace the pages of barbarian history. It would seem bad enough that this man should escape justice; but now comes his application for pardon, with the much-abused oath of allegiance, all in due form, presented in the coolest possible manner, with the humiliating endorsement of the highest officer in our army, urging that the pardon asked for shall be granted.*

Grant's conduct in the case, to the disgusted colonel, only showed that "the highest functionaries of this country are stooping from their lofty position of vindicating authority to the degrading condition of compounding with treason and taking from the basest of crimes its legitimate sting."[9]

Those who felt as Hawkins could only have been further enraged when on Christmas Day in 1868, President Johnson issued a proclamation extending "unconditionally and without reservation to all and to every person who directly or indirectly participated in the late insurrection or rebellion a full pardon and amnesty for the offense of treason against the U.S., or for adhering to their enemies during the civil war, with the restoration of all their civil rights, privileges and immunities under the Constitution...."[10]

Grant's support for Pickett did not end with helping him through the Kinston mess. It continued after he was elected president. George and Sally became welcome visitors to the White House where they were saluted and served by the staff with all the pomp accorded royal emissaries. On one occasion, the president offered Pickett the marshalship of the State of Virginia. "You cannot afford to do this," Pickett responded to the offer, "and I cannot afford to accept it from you."

"I can afford to do whatever I choose, Pickett," Grant gruffly reminded him.[11]

In an attempt to continue practicing the military profession, the only work they knew, many ex-Confederate officers were accepting army commissions abroad, particularly those being extended by Emperor Maximilian in Mexico. When an offer came from the Khedive of Egypt to be a brigadier general in his army — one his First Corps compatriot, Gen. Charles Field, had already accepted — Pickett declined. He did not wish to leave his country again. He would have to find other work.

Finally, as many others were doing, Pickett agreed to use his name as an entry to sell insurance, becoming general agent in Virginia for the Washington Life Insurance Company of New York. It was an undertaking in which he was only modestly successful and one he found not particularly stimulating. Whether due to ill health or abuse, George altered markedly in appearance and although only in his 40s during the Reconstruction years, he took on a worn, haggard look. Soon there was little trace of the jauntiness and dash he had affected as a troop commander.

Only once during the short period they survived the war did Pickett encounter General Lee and it was obvious that the latter had not forgotten or forgiven George's performance at Five Forks. Col. John S. Mosby, the partisan raider, happened to be in Richmond on March 8, 1870 and encountered Lee and his daughter, Agnes, on

the bridge connecting the Ballard and Exchange hotels. While chatting, the general said he was on his way to Savannah for his health and, in fact, "looked very badly."

A few minutes later, by sheer coincidence, Mosby ran into Pickett at the Exchange lobby and George said that if Mosby would accompany him he would go and pay his respects to Lee but "did not want to be alone with him." His reasoning evidently, in Mosby's view, was that Lee was a man of too much breeding to bring up any "unpleasant memories" of a confidential nature in the presence of a third party.

Their meeting, in Mosby's words, was "cold and formal" and terminated in less than five minutes (to the relief of all involved) by Miss Lee entering the room.[12] When they were outside, Pickett muttered bitterly. "That old man, he had my division massacred at Gettysburg." Mosby, perhaps a bit shocked to hear the exalted Lee spoken of in that tone, reflected a moment before responding: "Well, it made you immortal."[13]

Mosby noticed that Pickett was still in the office when Lee came down with his baggage but "he didn't go with us to the carriage and did not even say to him good-bye." At the time, Mosby said he was very slightly acquainted with Pickett and "knew nothing of his differences with Gen. Lee." Later he was to hear a former Confederate brigadier tell him that Pickett was in such disfavor at army headquarters that Col. Charles Marshall, Lee's assistant adjutant general, asserted that "Lee ought to have had Pickett shot."[14]

Another painful emotional experience awaited Pickett in June 1872 when the remains of 708 Confederate soldiers killed at Gettysburg were returned to Richmond for reburial at Hollywood Cemetery. The bodies were carried up to the historic cemetery in a mass funeral procession of wagons draped with Confederate flags and covered with flowers. Flags were flown at half-staff. A good many of the dead were removed from the Codori Farm at Gettysburg over which Pickett's Division had advanced and probably included the unidentified remains of one of his brigadiers, Richard B. Garnett.

Pickett had consented to join in the ceremony and walked behind the procession as an escort, reliving the last time he had been with these men advancing toward another cemetery in a far off Pennsylvania town. It was the same position, too, that he had occupied on the previous ascent.

(Virginia Historical Society)

George E. Pickett, after the war.

In the summer of 1875, Pickett and his wife were about to leave on a visit to White Sulphur Spring. Instead, some business crisis at the insurance agency of his brother, Charles, in Norfolk, Va., that George supervised erupted and the situation demanded that he go there immediately. While staying at the Atlantic Hotel, he was stricken and hurried to St. Vincent de Paul Hospital where he expired on August 5. He was 50 years old. The cause of death, according to the certificate, was abscess of the liver, a determination not surprising given Pickett's life style and demeanor.[15]

The Norfolk *Virginian* rushed into print a two-column obituary of the general, presented under a headline that read DEATH OF GEN. GEO. E. PICKETT, THE HERO OF GETTYSBURG. This notice began, "It is our painful duty to chronicle this morning the death of one of Virginia's noble sons...."

While nowhere in the account could be found any mention of the New Bern operation or Kinston, elsewhere on the page there was, by sheer coincidence, a reference in a social note of Pickett's old nemesis, Benjamin Butler. The Southern correspondent had found that still-hated figure at a New Hampshire regatta the day Pickett was expiring and reported that, "as might be expected 'Old Cock-Eye' Butler was the center of a group, listening to his stale and smutty jokes, and he as smiling and agreeable as it was possible to be. He has on his yacht 18 picked men, to whom it is said he pays $5 a day to escort him around the coast during the summer and thus the 'spoon' money and other 'war pickings' are spent by this 'disgrace to humanity.'"

Pickett's body was returned to Richmond for burial at Hollywood Cemetery among the South's most revered military leaders. To his young widow, of course, it was the grandest funeral anyone had ever seen. Suffice it to say that Pickett received his full measure of glory. His remains were accorded far more respect than was extended the stripped bodies deposited in the sand beneath the gallows at Kinston.

To the throng at his bier, and millions more throughout the South, Pickett was a symbol, the man who had carried their hopes on that fateful day at Gettysburg, the leader who had directed the supreme effort to accomplish their cause. History would have it no other way. Never mind the New Bern debacle, the breakdown at Petersburg and the dereliction at Five Forks. And never mind those 22 young North Carolinians put to death for declining to join in the secession movement. Pickett's place was secure, as Mosby so correctly observed. Anyone who had been so prominently associated with an event as awesome as that charge was bound to be forever elevated by the experience. When all is considered, however, it does sometimes seem that fate had made an unlikely choice in deciding that it was to be George E. Pickett who would give it its name.

Left without income by her husband's death, Sally, imaginative and ever resourceful, turned to writing to earn her living and to further enhance her husband's fame. In addition to publishing six books and numerous magazine articles (demonstrating a particular ability to capture Southern dialects) she became a popular figure on the lecture circuit, a charming fixture at the conventions of such groups as the United Confederate Veterans and the United Daughters of the Confederacy. Where memory failed or the facts seemed too distasteful or unchivalrous to suit her image

of her gallant husband's life, she improvised or invented and didn't mind at all drawing on the writings of others to improve the appeal and salability of her works.

Washington, D. C., became Sally's long-time place of residence. For many years she shared a unit of the Ontario Apartments with Mary Elizabeth Torrance, who helped her with her writing.

In 1889, in far off Portland, Oregon, a talented newspaper illustrator and promising painter died of tuberculosis at the age of 32 in a rooming house where he lived alone. Among his few belongings was a red leather trunk ornamented with rows of brass headed tacks, that had belonged to his Haida mother. The artist's name was James Tilton Pickett and inside the trunk were a number of worn personal letters and documents. The articles included the ceremonial gloves his parents had worn at their wedding, resolutions tendering thanks to Captain Pickett from the U. S. Congress for his stand at San Juan Island, his commission as a captain of the U. S. Army and some tintype pictures of the captain and his son. There was also a Bible in which had been written, "May the memory of your Mother, always remain dear. Your Father, George E. Pickett."

It was said that a number of letters from the general had been removed from James' room while the funeral services were being conducted as well as his most prized possession, a saber he claimed to be the one worn by his father at Gettysburg. But one packet of letters left untouched was a set of 13 from his step-mother, LaSalle Corbell Pickett.[16]

Although in her published writings she had disguised James' identity, referring to him as the child a chief had presented to Pickett as a gesture of fondness, she had, in fact, for years carried on an affectionate correspondence with the young man since his father's death. She had even given him the deed to some land her late husband had purchased in Whatcom, Washington, back in 1858.

During the Spanish-American War, it gave the lively widow deep satisfaction to see President McKinley extend a commission in the U. S. Army to her son, re-establishing a tradition that would in time see Picketts once more joining the long gray line at West Point. In fact, so elevated did the Pickett name become in the regular army that in 1942 a vast, 45,000 acre installation in the area in which he had fought as a Confederate leader was dedicated in his honor, and named Camp Pickett, Virginia.

In 1897—still 35 years before her own death but 34 years after the event with which her husband would always be linked, Sally decided to visit Gettysburg. There she gazed for the first time over

the immense open field across which her soldier's troops had advanced, a scene she had so often conjured. In her vivid imagination, Sally could—as she stood alone at the edge of the hallowed ground—no doubt see him there now, out in front, shining saber raised, his beautiful hair flowing in the breeze, exhorting his men to follow him right to the very mouths of the death-spewing guns. From her viewpoint, one formed by years of unabashed adulation, that was, after all, the only way it could have been.

LaSalle Corbell Pickett, in later years.

History's assessment

In Kinston today, when strolling along broad Queen Street, with its uniformly placed cone-shaped trees providing a measure of shade, one encounters no plaques or monuments to indicate that anything unusual occurred there during the War Between the States. Local histories at the public library contain no mention whatever of any executions having taken place there. The featured historical display the town offers is the worn hull of the ill-fated Confederate ram *Neuse* salvaged from the mud of the river in 1961 and moved on to the bank as a visitors attraction.

There is no special burial plot for the 22 Union soldiers hanged there; their bodies are dispersed to family burial grounds deep in the dark, pine bogs from which the men emerged. But how should such an episode as this be appropriately commemorated? In either uniform, the condemned men were indifferent soldiers at best. It would be absurd to suggest that the course they took was out of deep patriotic conviction. Their case is almost one of the nature of the crime eclipsing the victim, as when a flag of truce is violated no matter who the bearer.

To men such as Rush Hawkins and Gen. John J. Peck, so appalled that any man wearing the insignia of the Federal army would be executed by an armed force of rebels, the question of what these men had done before joining their ranks was of no consequence. To them, it was the United States government that was being insulted.

To George Pickett there probably was no matter of high principle involved in his actions. He behaved in a coldly pragmatic manner and dealt with what he considered a serious problem of discipline in the way he had been schooled to address such situations — harshly and decisively. Any officer reluctant to go as far in punishing deserters, he probably would have regarded as lacking his commitment to duty and not fulfilling his responsibility.

The Confederate army was on the verge of disintegrating. Tough measures had to be taken to hold it together. Desertions were weakening enough; if these defectors were to go over to the Union side in any numbers, it could be disastrous, Pickett reasoned. On his own,

in independent command, he dealt with the situation in a way he would have been restrained from doing when under the direct influence of a Lee or a Longstreet.

In the end, the values represented in the Kinston affair became rather hopelessly confused. Motives were ascribed to the executed that were far loftier than they deserved. High-ranking regular army officers would undermine their own service's board of inquiry by helping the subject to avoid its jurisdiction. Confederate soldiers sent to round up the deserters went over to the enemy. West Point-trained officers who had violated solemn oaths of allegiance by joining in the insurrection would become participants in the executions.

And where was justice? Was Pickett wrong to take the extreme steps he did?

History clearly has rendered its verdict in the matter. "As gallant as Pickett's Charge" has become a common military superlative and the image developed of the man assumed to have led it has been steadily enhanced as knowledge and appreciation of the enormity of that event grows.

Conversely, Pickett's involvement in what happened in Kinston that melancholy winter of 1864 has, deservedly or not, faded deeper into obscurity, disregarded by subsequent generations far more attracted by glorious deeds.

Notes

Chapter One:
Opportunity at New Bern

1. E. Porter Alexander, *Southern Historical Society Papers* (Richmond, VA: 1876-1930), Vol. 4, 105. Hereafter cited as *SHSP*.
2. Clifford Dowdey, *Death of a Nation* (New York: Alfred A. Knopf, 1958), 270.
3. George E. Pickett, *Soldier of the South* (Boston: Houghton, Mifflin Co., 1928), 60.
4. D. E. Johnston, *The Story of a Confederate Boy in the Civil War* (Portland, OR: Glass & Prudhomme Co., 1914), 205-206.
5. Rawley Martin, *SHSP,* Vol. 32, 186.
6. LaSalle Corbell Pickett, *Pickett and His Men* (Philadelphia and London: J. B. Lippencott Co., 1913), 302. Hereafter cited as *Mrs. Pickett.*
7. Randolph A. Shotwell, *Our Living and Dead* (Raleigh: 1874-1876), Vol. 4, 90.
8. William Youngblood, *SHSP,* Vol. 38, 317.
9. Francis W. Dawson, *Reminiscences of Confederate Service* (Baton Rouge: Louisiana State University Press, 1980), 97.
10. C. T. Loehr, *War History of the Old First Virginia Infantry Regiment* (Richmond, VA: Ellis Jones, 1884), 38.
11. *Mrs. Pickett,* 317.
12. John W. Daniel Papers, Clayton Coleman to Daniel, July 1, 1904, University of Virginia Library, Charlottesville, VA.
13. Raphael J. Moses Reminiscences, Manuscript Division, North Carolina Department of Archives and History, Raleigh, NC.
14. *Ibid.*
15. G. Moxley Sorrel, *Recollections of a Confederate Staff Officer* (Jackson, TN: McCowat-Mercer Press, 1958), 156. Hereafter cited as *Sorrel.*
16. George E. Pickett, *Heart of a Soldier* (New York: Seth Moyle, Inc., 1913), 2. Hereafter cited as *Pickett.* Although a New York *Times* obituary on March 23, 1931 gives her birthdate as May 16, 1848 as does a *Who's Who in America* listing, placing her at the age she used in her writing, Dr. Richard Selcer, a Pickett biographer, recently found that the Pickett marriage license from the city of Petersburg, and dated Sept. 15, 1863, gives her age as 19. Also, the 1860 census report from Nansemond County, Va., lists her as being sixteen at that time.
17. *Ibid.,* 3.
18. *Ibid.,* 3-4.

19. *Ibid.*, 4.

20. Lelah Jackson Edson, *The Fourth Corner — Highlights from the Early Northwest* (Bellingham, WA: Whatcom Museum of History and Art, 1968), 116. Hereafter cited as *Edson.*

21. *Pickett,* 5.

22. *Edson,* 117.

23. *Ibid.*, 117.

24. Randolph A. Shotwell, *The Papers of . . .,* edited by J. G. de R. Hamilton, (Raleigh, NC: North Carolina Historical Commission, 1929), 170.

25. Bernhard Domschcke, *Twenty Months in Captivity: Memoirs of a Union Officer in Confederate Prisons* (Rutherford, NJ: Fairleigh Dickinson University Press, 1987), 29-30.

26. *Pickett,* 213.

27. *Official Records of the Union and Confederate Armies,* Vol. 29, Part 2, 773-774. Hereafter cited as *OR.*

28. *OR.*, Vol. 29, Part 2, 706.

29. *Pickett,* 11.

30. *Ibid.*, 11-12.

31. *OR.* 29, Part 2, 773-774.

32. E. W. Gaines, *SHSP* (Richmond, VA: 1876-1930), Vol. 25, 288. Hereafter cited as *Gaines.*

33. *OR.*, Vol. 33, 1061.

34. *OR.*, Vol. 23, 950-951.

35. Georgia Lee Tatum, *Disloyalty in the Confederacy* (Chapel Hill, NC: University of North Carolina Press, 1934), 125.

36. *OR.*, Vol. 33, 1102-1103.

37. *Sorrel,* 48.

38. *Gaines,* 289.

39. Henry W. Thomas, *History of the Doles-Cook Brigade* (Dayton, OH: Press of Morningside Bookshop, 1988), 358. Hereafter cited as *Thomas.*

40. James Cooper Nisbet, *4 Years on the Firing Line* (Jackson, TN: McCowat-Mercer Press, 1963), 13. Hereafter cited as *Nisbet.*

41. *Ibid.*, 72.

42. *Thomas,* 349.

43. John R. La Rogue Papers, University of Georgia Libraries, Manuscript Collection, Athens, GA.

44. *Executive Document No. 98,* U. S. House of Representatives, Thirty-ninth Congress, 68. Hereafter cited as *E. D.*

**Chapter Two:
"Rebellion Seems to be Expensive"**

1. T. C. Johnson, *The Story of Kinston and Lenoir County* (Raleigh, NC: Edwards & Broughton Co., 1954), 99.

2. *Ibid.*

3. Henry Thomas Kennon Papers, letter of June 9, 1863. Manuscript Division, North Carolina Department of Archives and History, Raleigh, NC.

4. William F. Loftin Papers, letter of Jan. 3, 1861. Manuscript Division, Perkins Library, Duke University, Durham, NC.

5. Samuel P. Lockhart Papers, letter of May 11, 1862. Manuscript Division, Perkins Library, Duke University, Durham, NC.

6. Tarboro *Southerner,* Jan. 17, 1863.

7. Mrs. Martha Ellen Miller, *North Carolina Historical*

Review, Vol. 5 (1928), 454. Hereafter cited as *Miller*.

8. *Carolina and the Southern Cross*, Vol.1, 1912. Hereafter cited as *CSC*.

9. Lalla Pelot Papers, letter from W. W. Sullivan dated Dec. 27, 1862. Manuscript Division, Perkins Library, Duke University, Durham, NC.

10. *Ibid.*

11. *Miller*, 454.

12. Zeuas T. Haines, *Letters from the Massachusetts 44th Regiment* (Boston: Boston Herald Company, 1863), 45. Hereafter cited as *Haines*.

13. Samuel H. Putnam, *The Story of Co. A, 25th Massachusetts Volunteers* (Worcester, MA: Putnam, Davis & Co., 1886), 116. Hereafter cited as *Putnam*.

14. *Haines*, 55.

15. *Putnam*, 146.

16. David L. Day, *My Diary of Rambles with the 25th Massachusetts Volunteers* (Milford, MA: King and Billings, 1884), 80. Hereafter cited as *Day*.

17. *Haines*, 56-57.

18. *Putnam*, 147.

19. *Miller,* 455.

20. *CSC*, Vol. 1, 1912.

21. *Miller*, 456-457.

22. *Day*, 80.

23. *Putnam*, 147.

24. *Ibid.*, 148.

25. *CSC*, Vol. 1, 1913.

26. R. H. Bacot Papers, letter of March 19, 1864. Manuscript Division, North Carolina Department of Archives and History, Raleigh, NC. Hereafter cited as *Bacot*.

27. Frontis W. Johnston, ed., *Papers of Zebulon B. Vance* (Raleigh, NC: North Carolina Depart-

ment of Archives and History, 1963), Vol. 1, 286.

28. William H. Cocke Papers, letter of Oct. 21, 1863. Virginia Historical Society, Richmond, VA. Hereafter cited as *Cocke*.

29. Benjamin H. Sims Journal, Manuscript Division, North Carolina Department of Archives and History, Raleigh, NC. Hereafter cited as *Sims*.

30. Hodijah Lincoln Meade Papers, letter of Feb. 9, 1864. Virginia Historical Society, Richmond, VA. Hereafter cited as *Meade*.

31. Capt. Charles W. Squires, *Civil War Times Illustrated*, May-June 1975. Hereafter cited as *Squires*.

32. Capt. Sidney J. Richardson Papers, letter of Feb. 5, 1864. Georgia Department of Archives and History, Atlanta, Ga.

33. *OR.*, Vol. 33, 96.

34. *Ibid.*, 96.

35. *Ibid.*, 93-94.

36. *Squires.*

37. J. L. Stuart Papers, letter of Feb. 5, 1864. Manuscript Division, Perkins Library, Duke University, Durham, NC. Hereafter cited as *Stuart*.

38. *OR.*, Vol. 33, 94.

39. *Stuart*, letter of Feb. 5, 1864.

40. *Squires.*

41. Capt. Henry A. Chambers Diary, Feb. 3, 1864. Manuscript Division, North Carolina Department of Archives and History, Raleigh, NC.

42. *OR.*, Vol. 33, 94.

43. *Ibid.*, 93-94.

44. *Ibid.*, 96-97.

45. *Capt. John G. Smith, CSC*, Vol. 2, 1914. Hereafter cited as *Smith*.

46. *Thomas*, 359.

47. Walter Harrison, *Pickett's Men* (New York: D. Van Nostrand, 1870), 117. Hereafter cited as *Harrison*.

Chapter Three:
"An awful cold, bad day"
1. *E. D.*, 80.
2. Wilmington *Journal*, April 28, 1864.
3. *E. D.*, 34.
4. *Richardson*, letter of Feb. 5, 1864.
5. *OR.*, V. 33, 866-867.
6. *Ibid.*, 867-868.
7. *Ibid.*, 867.
8. *Ibid.*, 867-868.
9. Rush L. Hawkins, *An Account of the Assassination of Loyal Citizens of North Carolina* (New York: J. H. Folan, 1897), 38. Hereafter cited as *Hawkins*.
10. *Harrison*, 118.
11. *Ibid.*
12. *Smith.*
13. *E. D.*, 46.
14. *Harrison*, 117.
15. *E. D.*, 32.
16. *E. D.*, 30.
17. *E. D.*, 39.
18. *E. D.*, 13-14.
19. Leonidas Polk Papers, letter of Feb. 13, 1864. Manuscript Division, North Carolina Department of Archives and History, Raleigh, NC. Hereafter cited as *Polk.*
20. *E. D.*, 41.
21. *Gaines.*
22. *E. D.*, 69.
23. *Smith.*
24. *Polk*, letter of Feb. 13, 1864.
25. *E. D.*, 14.
26. *E. D.*, 30.
27. *E. D.*, 46.
28. *E. D.*, 28.
29. *E. D.*, 31.
30. Montgomery D. Corse, *Biography of Gen. Montgomery D. Corse.* Prepared by his son and circulated privately. On file at Lloyd House, Library of Virginia History & Genealogy, Alexandria, VA, 47.
31. *E. D.*, 41.
32. *E. D.*, 36.
33. *E. D.*, 68.
34. *Polk*, letter of Feb. 13, 1864.
35. Henry J. H. Thompson Papers, letter of April 3, 1864. Manuscript Division, Perkins Library, Duke University, Durham, NC.
36. *Bacot*, letter of Jan. 18, 1865.
37. Herman W. Taylor Papers, letter of William Dixon Carr dated Feb. 22, 1864. Manuscript Division, North Carolina Department of Archives and History, Raleigh, NC.
38. *Cocke*, letter of Oct. 21, 1863.
39. *Ibid.*, letter of Dec. 14, 1863.
40. *Meade*, letter of Feb. 4, 1864.
41. G. Howard Gregory, *The 38th Virginia Infantry* (Lynchburg, VA: H. E. Howard, Inc., 1988), 48.
42. Robert K. Krick, *The 30th Virginia Infantry* (Lynchburg, VA: H. E. Howard, Inc., 1983), 47.
43. *Ibid.*
44. *E. D.*, 40.
45. *E. D.*, 13.
46. *OR.*, Vol. 33, 868.
47. *Ibid.*, 869-870.
48. Benjamin F. Butler, *Private and Official Correspondence of . . . during the period of the Civil War* (privately issued), Vol. 4, 424-425.
49. *Ibid.*, 146.
50. The Rev. John Paris, *A Sermon Preached Before Brigadier General Hoke's Brigade at*

Kinston, N. C., on the 28th of Feb., 1864 (Goldsboro, NC: Privately printed, 1864).

Chapter Four:
"Is That Man Still With This Army?"
1. *Hawkins*, 9-10.
2. *Ibid.*, 3.
3. *Ibid.*, 28.
4. *OR.*, Vol. 33, 948-949.
5. *Ibid.*, 92.
6. *OR.*, Vol. 59, 994.
7. *OR.*, Vol. 51, Part 2, 857.
8. *Pickett*, 187.
9. *Mrs. Pickett*, 344.
10. Josiah Gorgas, *The Civil War Diary of ...*, Frank E. Vandiver, ed. (University, AL: University of Alabama Press, 1947), May 10, 1864; *Braxton Bragg Papers.*
11. J. P. Alderman, *The 29th Virginia Regiment* (Lynchburg, VA: H. E. Howard, Inc., 1987), 48.
12. John S. Wise, *The End of an Era,* 338. Hereafter cited as *Wise.*
13. *Pickett*, 167.
14. *Wise,* 338.
15. William B. Randolph Papers, letter of Nov. 6, 1864. Manuscript Division, Library of Congress, Washington, D.C.
16. *Pickett*, 139.
17. *Ibid.*, 19.
18. George E. Pickett Papers, letter from Gen. Robert E. Lee to Gen. James Longstreet regarding Pickett's Division, Jan. 19, 1865.
19. *O. R.*, V. 42, part 3, 1213.
20. *Mrs. Pickett,* 367-370.
21. *O. R.*, V. 46, Pt. 3, 1332.
22. *O. R.*, V. 29, Pt. 2, 873.
23. *Mrs. Pickett,* 386.
24. Proceedings of the Court of Inquiry in the case of Gouverneur K. Warren, U. S. War Department, Washington, D. C., 481.
25. Thomas T. Munford MSS.
26. Armistead L. Long, *Memoirs of Robert E. Lee,* (New York: J. M. Stoddart & Co., 1886), 410.
27. Catherine Ann Devereux Edmonson, *The Journal of a Secesh Lady* (Raleigh, NC: North Carolina Department of Cultural Resources, Division of Archives and History, 1979), 705.
28. Douglas S. Freeman, *R. E. Lee* (New York and London: Charles Scribner's Sons, 1935), Vol. 4, 112.
29. Henry E. Tremain, *Last Hours of Sheridan's Cavalry* (New York: Bonnell, Silver and Bowers, 1904), 266.
30. Charles Carleton Coffin, *The Boys of '61 or Four Years of Fighting* (Boston: Estes and Lauriat, 1883), 553-554.
31. *Mrs. Pickett, 4.*
32. *Pickett,* 15-16.
33. *Ibid.,* 17.

Chapter Five:
"Crimes too Heinous to be Excused"
1. *Pickett,* 49.
2. *Mrs. Pickett,* 22-25.
3. *Hawkins,* 34-35.
4. Orville Hickman Browning, *The Diary of . . .,* James G. Randall, ed., (Springfield, IL: Illinois State Historical Library, 1926) Vol. 2, (1865-1881), 48.
5. *Ibid.,* 48-49.
6. Margaret Leech, *Reville in Washington* (New York: Grosset & Dunlap, 1941), 410.
7. *Ibid.,* 159.
8. *Hawkins,* 36.

9. *Mrs. Pickett*, 428.
10. *Ibid.*, 30.
11. *Ibid.*
12. *Ibid.* Mrs. Pickett's journey to Montreal and her arrival there are related in 33-64.
13. *E. D.*, 14.
14. *E. D.*, 28
15. *E. D.*, 30.
16. *Ibid.*
17. *Ibid.*
18. *E. D.*, 33.
19. *E. D.*, 36.
20. *E. D.*, 38-39.
21. Robert K. Krick, *Lee's Colonels* (Dayton, OH: Press of Morningside Bookshop, 1979), 248.
22. *E. D.*, 41.
23. *Ibid.*
24. *E. D.*, 42.
25. *E. D.*, 13-17.
26. *E. D.*, 48-49.
27. *E. D.*, 53-54.
28. *E. D.*, 55.
29. *Hawkins*, 32.
30. *E. D.*, 55.
31. *E. D.*, 61.
32. *E. D.*, 62-63.
33. *E. D.*, 67.
34. *E. D.*, 68-70.
35. *E. D.*, 71.
36. *E. D.*, 72.
37. *E. D.*, 73-74.
38. *E. D.*, 76-77.
39. *E. D.*, 78-79.
40. *E. D.*, 55-59.
41. *E. D.*, 52-53.

Chapter Six:
"But He Made You Immortal"
1. This final phase of the Picketts' stay in Canada is described in *Mrs. Pickett, 77-85.*
2. *Browning, 48-49.*
3. *Pickett*, 20-21.
4. *Mrs. Pickett*, 85.
5. *Pickett*, 20-21.
6. *Hawkins*, 37-38.
7. *Ibid.*, 39.
8. John Y. Simon, ed., *The Papers of U. S. Grant* (Carbondale and Edwardsville, IL: Southern Illinois University Press, 1991), Vol. 17, 221.
9. *Hawkins*, 33-34.
10. New York *Times,* Jan. 19, 1869.
11. *Mrs. Pickett,* 428.
12. *John S. Mosby Papers*, letter to Eppa Hunton, March 25, 1911. Virginia Historical Society, Richmond, VA.
13. *John S. Mosby Memoirs*, Charles W. Russell, ed. (Boston: Little, Brown & Co., 1917), 380-381.
14. Mosby letter.
15. Jack D. Welsh, M.D., *Medical Histories of Confederate Generals* (Kent, OH and London: Kent State University Press, 1995), 172.
16. *Edson*, 120.

Bibliography

Sources for this work have been grouped in four categories: General Works, Manuscripts and Letters, Periodicals and Collections and Newspapers.

General Works

Alderman, J. P. *The 29th Virginia Regiment.* Lynchburg, Va.: H. E. Howard, Inc., 1987.

Barrett, John G. *The Civil War in North Carolina.* Chapel Hill, NC: University of North Carolina Press, 1963.

Butler, Benjamin F. *Private and Official Correspondence of General Benjamin F. Butler during the period of the Civil War.* Privately issued, 1917.

Coffin, Charles Carleton. *The Boys of '61 or Four Years of Fighting.* Boston: Estes and Lauriat, 1883.

Corse, Montgomery D. *Biography of Gen. Montgomery D. Corse.* Prepared by his son and circulated privately. Copy presented to Lloyd House, Library of Virginia History & Genealogy, Alexandria Va., by his grandson, Rear Admiral Albert C. Murdaugh (Ret.) in 1969.

Day, David L. *My Diary of Rambles with the 25th Massachusetts Volunteers.* Milford, Ma.: King & Billings, 1884.

Dowdey, Clifford. *Death of a Nation: The Story of Lee and His Men at Gettysburg.* New York: Alfred A. Knopf, 1958.

Edmunson, Catherine Ann Devereux. *The Journal of a Secesh Lady.* Raleigh: North Carolina Department of Cultural Resources, Division of Archives & History, 1979.

Edson, Lelah Jackson. *The Fourth Corner: Highlights from the Early Northwest.* Bellingham, Wa.: Whatcom Museum of History & Art, 1968.

Freeman, Douglas Southall. *R. E. Lee: A Biography.* 4 Vols., New York and London: Charles Scribner's Sons, 1935.

Gregory, G. Howard. *The 38th Virginia Regiment.* Lynchburg, Va.: H. E. Howard, Inc., 1988.

Gunn, Ralph White. *The 24th Virginia Regiment.* Lynchburg, Va.: H. E. Howard, Inc., 1987.

Haines, Zeuas T. *Letters from the Massachusetts 44th Regiment.* Boston: Boston Herald Company, 1863.

Hamilton, J. G. de R. and Rebecca Cameron, eds. *The Papers of Randolph A. Shotwell.* 3 vols. Raleigh: North Carolina Historical Commission, 1929.

Harrison, Walter. *Pickett's Men: A Fragment of War History.* New York: D. Van Nostrand, 1870.

Hawkins, Rush L. *An Account of the Assassination of Loyal Citizens of North Carolina.* New York: J. H. Folan, 1897.

Inman, Arthur Crew, ed. *Soldier of the South: Pickett's War Letters to His Wife.* Boston: Houghton, Mifflin Co., 1928.

Johnson, Talmage C. and Charles R. Holloman. *The Story of Kinston and Lenoir County.* Raleigh: Edwards & Broughton Co., 1954.

Johnston, D. E. *The Story of a Confederate Boy in the Civil War.* Portland, Or.: Glass & Prudhomme Co., 1914.

Johnston, Frontis W., ed. *The Papers of Zebulon B. Vance.* Raleigh: North Carolina Department of Archives and History, 1963.

Krick, Robert K. *Lee's Colonels: A Biographical Register of the Field Officers of the Army of Northern Virginia.* Dayton, Oh: Press of Morningside Bookshop, 1979.

Krick, Robert K. *The 30th Virginia Regiment.* Lynchburg, Va.: H. E. Howard, Inc., 1983.

Leech, Margaret. *Reville in Washington.* New York: Grosset & Dunlap, 1941.

Loehr, C. T. *War History of the Old First Virginia Infantry Regiment, Army of Northern Virginia.* Richmond: Ellis Jones, 1884.

Long, Armistead L. *Memoirs of Robert E. Lee.* New York: J. M. Stoddart & Co., 1886.

Pickett, LaSalle Corbell, ed. *Heart of a Soldier: Pickett's War Letters to His Wife.* New York: Seth Moyle, Inc., 1913.

_____. *Pickett and His Men.* Philadelphia and London: J. B. Lippincott Co., 1913.

_____. *What Happened to Me.* New York: Brentano's, 1917.

Powell, William S. *Annals of Progress: The Story of Lenoir County and Kinston, N. C.* Raleigh: North Carolina Department of Archives & History, 1963.

Putnam, Samuel H. *The Story of Co. A, 25th Massachusetts Volunteers.* Worcester, Ma.: Putnam, Davis & Co., 1886.

Randall, James G., ed. *The Diary of Orville Hickman Browning.* Springfield, Il.: Illinois State Historical Library, 1926.

Russell, Charles W., ed. *Memoirs of John S. Mosby.* Boston: Little, Brown & Co., 1917.

Tatum, Georgia Lee. *Disloyalty in the Confederacy*. Chapel Hill, N. C.: University of North Carolina Press, 1934.

Thomas, Henry W. *History of the Doles-Cook Brigade*. Dayton, Oh.: Press of Morningside Bookshop, 1988.

Trautmann, Frederick, ed. *Twenty Months in Captivity: Memoirs of a Union Officer in Confederate Prisons*. (Bernhard Domscheke) Rutherford, N.J.: Fairleigh Dickinson University Press, 1987.

Tremain, Henry E. *Last Hours of Sheridan's Cavalry*, New York: Bonnell, Silver and Bowers, 1904.

Vandiver, Frank E., ed. *The Civil War Diary of Gen. Josiah Gorgas*. University, Al.: University of Alabama Press, 1947.

Welsh, Jack D., M.D. *Medical Histories of Confederate Generals*. Kent, Oh., and London: Kent State University Press, 1995.

Wiley, Bell I., ed. *Reminiscences of Confederate Service, 1861-1865*. (Francis W. Dawson) Baton Rouge: Louisiana State University Press, 1980.

_____. *Four Years on the Firing Line*. (James C. Nisbet) Jackson, Tn.: McCowatMercer Press, 1963.

_____. *Recollections of a Confederate Staff Officer*. (G. Moxley Sorrel) Jackson, Tn.: McCowat-Mercer Press, 1958.

Wise, John S. *The End of an Era*. Boston: Houghton, Mifflin Co., 1899.

Manuscripts and Letters

Braxton Bragg Papers, Duke University, Durham, N. C.

R. H. Bacot Papers, Manuscript Division, North Carolina Department of Archives and History, Raleigh, N. C.

Henry A. Chambers Diary, Manuscript Division, North Carolina Department of Archives and History, Raleigh, N.C.

William H. Cocke Papers, Virginia Historical Society, Richmond, Va.

Montgomery D. Corse Papers, Lloyd House, Library of Virginia History & Genealogy, Alexandria, Va.

John W. Daniel Papers, University of Virginia Library, Charlottesville, Va.

Ulysses S. Grant Papers, John Y. Simon, ed., Carbondale and Edwardsville, Il: Southern Illinois University Press, 1991.

Thomas Kennon Papers, Manuscript Division, North Carolina Department of Archives and History, Raleigh, N. C.

John R. La Rogue Papers, University of Georgia Libraries, Manuscript Collection, Athens, Ga.

Samuel P. Lockhart Papers, Manuscript Division, Perkins Library, Duke University, Durham, N.C.

William F. Lotftin Papers, Manuscript Division, Perkins Library, Duke University, Durham, N.C.

Hodijah Lincoln Meade Papers, Virginia Historical Society, Richmond, Va.

John S. Mosby Papers, Virginia Historical Society, Richmond, Va.

Raphael J. Moses Reminiscences, Manuscript Division, North Carolina Department of Archives and History, Raleigh, N.C.

Thomas T. Munford Papers, Manuscript Division, Perkins Library, Duke University, Durham, N.C.

Lalla Pelot Papers, Manuscript Division, Perkins Library, Duke University, Durham, N.C.

Leonidas Polk Papers, Manuscript Division, North Carolina Department of Archives and History, Raleigh, N.C.

William B. Randolph Papers, Manuscript Division, Library of Congress, Washington, D. C.

Sidney J. Richardson Papers, Georgia Department of Archives and History, Atlanta, Ga.

Benjamin H. Sims Journal, Manuscript Division, North Carolina Department of Archives and History, Raleigh, N.C.

J. L. Stuart Papers, Manuscript Division, Perkins Library, Duke University, Durham, N.C.

Herman W. Taylor Papers, Manuscript Division, North Carolina Department of Archives and History, Raleigh, N.C.

Henry J. H. Thompson Papers, Manuscript Division, Perkins Library, Duke University, Durham, N.C.

Periodicals and Collections

Carolina and the Southern Cross, 1912-1913, Kinston, N. C.

Civil War Times Illustrated, Harrisburg, 1961

Histories of the Several Regiments and Battalions from North Carolina in the Great War, 1861-1865. Walter Clark, ed., Raleigh and Goldsboro, N.C.

North Carolina Historical Review, Raleigh, 1924

Our Living and Our Dead, Raleigh, 1874-76.

Photographic History of the Civil War. 10 vols. Francis Trevelyan Miller, editor-in-chief. Review of Reviews Co., New York, 1910.

Southern Historical Society Papers, 49 Vols. Richmond, 1876-1930.

U. S. War Department, *The War of the Rebellion: The Official Records of the Union and Confederate Armies,* 128 Vols. Washington, 1880-1901.

Newspapers
Charleston, S. C., *Courier*
Fayetteville, N. C., *Observer*
New York *Times*
Norfolk *Virginian*
Raleigh, North Carolina *Standard*
Raleigh, N. C., *Weekly Confederate*
Richmond *Examiner*
Wilmington, N. C., *Daily Journal*

Miscellaneous Material
U. S. Congress, House of Representatives, Executive Document 98, "Murder of Union Soldiers in North Carolina," Washington, 1866. (Transcript of two boards of inquiry.)
U. S. War Department, Proceedings of the Court of Inquiry in the case of Gen. Gouverneur K. Warren, Washington, 1879.

Index

About the Author

Gerard A. Patterson is the author of *Rebels From West Point* and has contributed some 30 articles to *Civil War Times Illustrated, American History,* and other history publications. A longtime newspaperman, Patterson retired in 1995 as associate editor of the Pittsburgh Post-Gazette to concentrate on Civil War research and writing. He is a resident of Mt. Lebanon, Pa.

THOMAS PUBLICATIONS publishes books about the American Colonial era, the Revolutionary War, the Civil War, and other important topics. For a list of titles, please see our web-site at http://civilwarreader.com/thomas.

Or write to:

THOMAS PUBLICATIONS
P.O. Box 3031
Gettysburg, PA 17325